Create That Change!

The Quest Toolbox Series

This series is different. It provides practical techniques, tested by experienced consultants with real organisations. Each tool follows a step-by-step approach, illustrated by worked examples. No theoretical explanations, just a wide choice of techniques to help stimulate, drive and manage change and the people that create it. Hundreds of directors, managers and team leaders worldwide are already using the series for personal reference, as handout material for training programmes or as an aid for project or improvement teams.

Steve Smith

Dr Smith has been helping organisations transform their performance and culture for 20 years. His unique experience of witnessing and consulting in global corporate change has helped him become regarded as one of the most progressive change management consultants of his generation.

A regular speaker and author, as well as conceptual thinker, Steve has facilitated the metamorphosis of over 150 organisations through the provision of timely, supportive and often pioneering consultancy advice.

A strong advocate of an holistic approach to business improvement, Steve works with his clients to define stretching, yet balanced strategies that work, and then helps to mobilise the whole organisation to turn those strategies into action.

Prior to forming Quest, Steve was a director of PA Consulting Services, where he worked for 11 years and founded the TQM division. A former lecturer at Aston University, Steve has also spent eight years with the Chrysler Corporation.

Acknowledgements

The Toolbox series has been drawn from the expertise of the entire Quest Worldwide consultancy team. Special thanks must go to Gillian Hayward for selecting and compiling tools for all five titles and to Mike Rayburn who developed and refined many of the techniques in *Make Things Happen!* Thanks also to Peter Holman, Tina Jacobs, Sue Hodder and the Quest support team.

Create That Change!

Readymade Tools for Change Management

Edited by
Steve Smith

KOGAN PAGE

QUEST QUALITY

South Asian Edition 1999, 2005

Kogan Page India Private Limited
2/13 Ansari Road
Daryaganj
New Delhi 110 002.

This edition is for sale in India, Bangladesh, Nepal, Pakistan and Sri Lanka only. Not for export elsewhere.

ISBN 81-7554-103-2

Published by Vinod Vasishtha for Kogan Page India Private Limited, 2/13 Ansari Road, Daryaganj, New Delhi - 110 002 and printed & bound at Raj Press, R-3 Inderpuri, New Delhi - 110 012.

Contents

Introduction

Change is a constant in our lives, both at work and at home. There are many drivers and influences behind change.

Together all of these forces have radically altered what we do; the way we do it and the environment in which we operate. Not all change is massive; there are also everyday incremental improvements in technology and organisation moving us in small steps towards a different world.

This Toolbox includes a range of practical tools which will help you to be a proactive leader and enthusiastic champion of change rather than a victim of circumstance.

HINT! REMEMBER: YOU REALLY CAN MAKE A DIFFERENCE IF YOU ONLY WANT TO!

How to use this Toolbox

What it is

This Toolbox is structured around the Quest model of effective change:

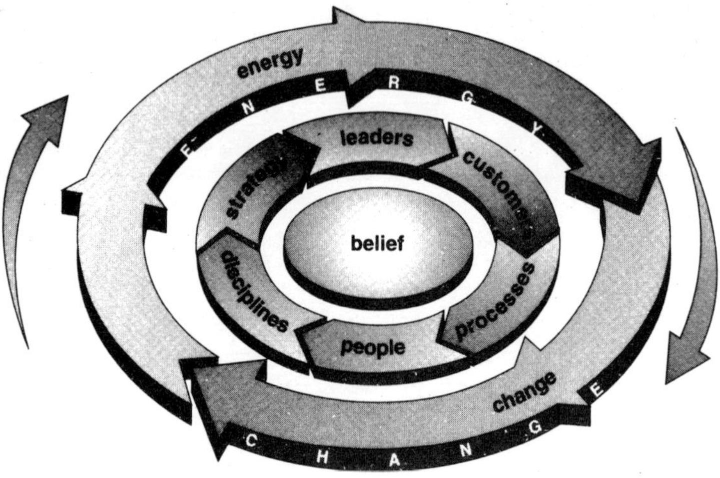

This model is outlined in the first section to give you a conceptual framework against which you can apply all of the other 'how to...' tools in the Toolbox.

For each tool, there is description of:

- What it is.
- How to use it.
- How it helps.

How to use it

1. Identify which driver you need to work on. ('Check your fitness for change' will help you to do this.)
2. Look through the index of the tools available.

3. Select the most appropriate tool.

4. Turn to the detailed tool description. The 'What it is' section explains the purpose of the tool; the 'How to use it' section gives you step by step instructions and the 'How it helps' section outlines the benefits of using the tool.

5. Go use it!

How it helps

Change can be very difficult. By breaking it down into the key drivers and identifying simple tools to implement each driver, this Toolbox will increase your success in 'Creating the difference.'

Tools index

1 Design for change

A Model for Change

What it is

Without a clear process to follow, change is haphazard and lacking foundation. This tool outlines a simple model developed by Quest to give shape to the transformation of an organisation from today's reality to tomorrow's vision:

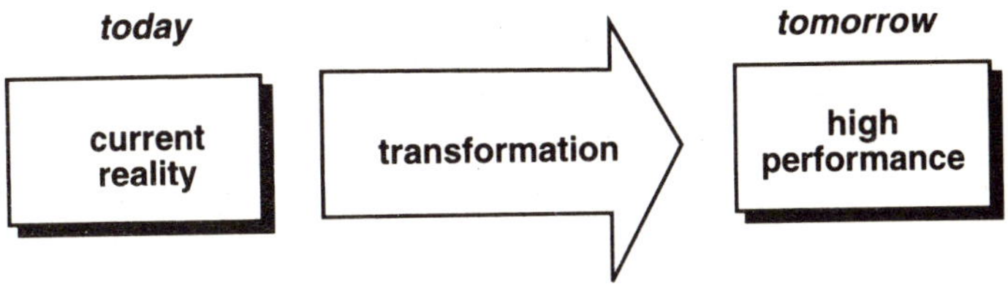

How to use it

1. Can you describe today's reality for your organisation? Do you know:

- what your customers think of you?
- how your processes really perform?
- how your people feel about their work?
- if you are getting the best out of all your resources?

If not, the tool on 'use facts' will help you decide what to do.

2. Are you clear where you want and need to get to? If not, refer to the next section on 'Start with belief'. Is your future sufficiently different to today to create a pressure or an energy for change? Will it enthuse and energise everyone?

3. Do you have a plan for achieving the change you need and building a culture which will sustain continuous improvement? If not, refer to the tools on developing a strategy.

4. If you are planning significant change, do you have resource you can commit to it or are you simply going to stretch what you've got even further? Are you clear about what you need, where it is coming from and what other, lower priorities will be dropped to free up resources?

5. So do you have all of the pre-requisites for change?

   - A need for change?
   - A vision of the future?
   - A forward plan?
   - Resource to implement change?

   Beware of what happens if any are missing:

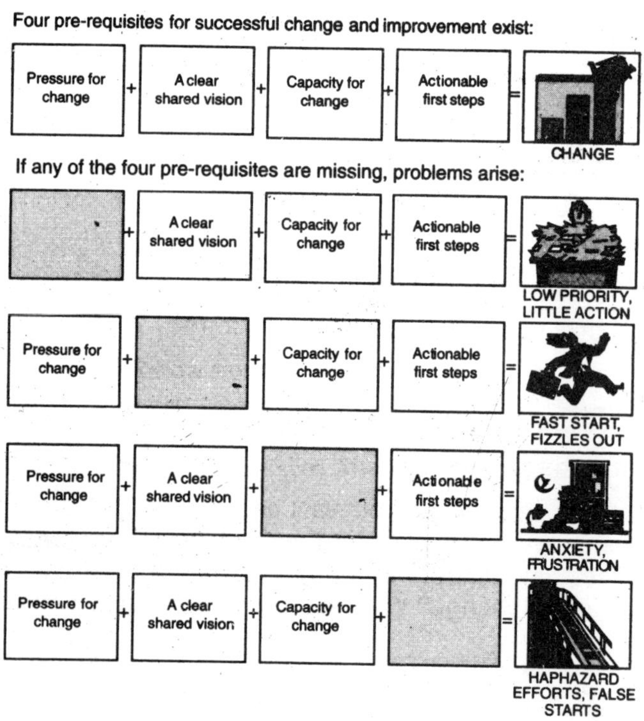

How it helps

Being clear about where you are going and how far away it is from today's reality are the first steps in approaching transformation. You also need a plan for how you are going to change and resource to do it with.

HINT!

DREAMS ALONE ARE NOT ENOUGH.
YOU NEED HARD FACTS AND CLEAR PLANS IF THEY
ARE TO BECOME REALITY

The Drivers for Change

What it is

The previous tool outlined a simple model for change. This tool goes on to break the transformation process down into the key drivers for change. Each of these is then broken down further in the remaining sections of the Toolbox.

The following diagram summarises the drivers, or forces, which you need to tackle and harness if you are going to bring about lasting change.

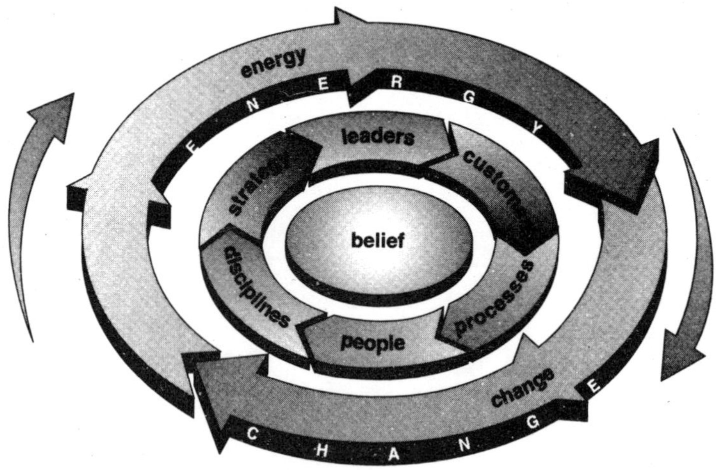

To be more specific, you need:

Belief: a defined philosophy, values and culture which are compatible with your vision for the future.

Strategy: clear goals, measures and targets in the areas which will lead to success.

Leaders: role models and champions to lead the way.

Customers: known customers with agreed needs.

Processes: efficient and effective methods and systems for producing agreed outputs.

People: who are equipped and energised to contribute.

Disciplines: techniques to approach tasks logically and effectively.

Energy: enthusiasm, creativity and will to succeed.

How to use it

1. Review the Quest drivers for change.
2. Which do you feel you have in place? Be specific about what/who you mean. Are you sure?
3. Where do you feel you have significant gaps?
4. Use the next tool 'Assess your fitness for change' to test your views.
5. This Toolbox is structured around the Quest drivers. Once you have identified your needs, use the tools to help you plan what to do.

How it helps

The Quest drivers give a structure and approach to planning and organising change. Use the model to assess your needs and focus your thoughts.

Check Your Fitness for Change

What it is

This tool allows you to quickly diagnose your organisation against the Quest model to establish your readiness for change.

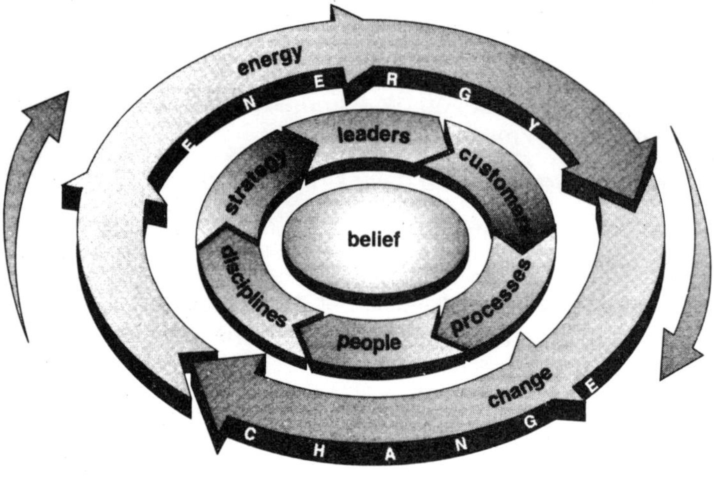

How to use it

1. Review the following questions. Answer honestly whether or not they describe your organisation as it is today.

Be tough on yourself and your company – if your immediate answer is 'not sure' or 'not everywhere', then tick 'No'!

Belief: setting the revolutionary mind-set

	Yes	No
• Is your belief in an overall improvement philosophy well understood across the business?	☐	☐
• Are you continually re-inventing the business to meet new market challenges and opportunities?	☐	☐

- Have you defined your market edge and are you anticipating shortfalls in performance? ☐ ☐
- Are you prepared to change anything and everything in order to maintain accelerated improvement? ☐ ☐
- Are you in it for the long term... that is, are you prepared for continuous revolution? ☐ ☐

Energy: generating improvement vitality to transform the business **Yes** **No**

- Are you explicitly managing the process of change? ☐ ☐
- Are you keeping the energy sources (champions, excitement, events, pace) well stoked up to power through blockages as they occur? ☐ ☐
- Are you continually attacking the energy sappers and watching out for new ones? ☐ ☐
- Are you, personally, setting a high energy example? ☐ ☐
- Have you converted the great unmoved... are they energised for improvement? ☐ ☐

Strategy: putting Quality behind business

Yes **No**

- Have you communicated the future practice of the organisation –what is valued and the way things should be done? ☐ ☐
- Have you created a clear strategic framework from an overall vision down to day-to-day behaviours? ☐ ☐

- Do you have stretch improvement goals which lead to a competitive edge, with clear measures to track progress? ☐ ☐
- Is your business plan live, with an active planning process top-down and bottom-up... do people use it to make decisions? ☐ ☐
- Is the improvement process fully intertwined with the business processes? ☐ ☐

Leadership: showing an example from the top

	Yes	**No**
• Are you personally a role model for the business?	☐	☐
• Are you both visionary and missionary, pointing the way and guiding people to get there?	☐	☐
• Has your commitment to tomorrow's business stood up to the test of today's?	☐	☐
• Are you able to let go and empower others beneath you?	☐	☐
• Do you have a personal development plan... that is, are you improving yourself?	☐	☐

Customers: aligning the business around customers' needs

	Yes	No
• Is 'customer' the big word in your business... the trigger for action?	☐	☐
• Does 'customer' mean something important everywhere in the business?	☐	☐
• Are you successfully and consistently managing customers' expectations and response to your service?	☐	☐
• Are you reading tomorrow's customer needs and preparing for them?	☐	☐
• Do your customers really need you?	☐	☐

Creating lean processes

	Yes	No
• Are processes more important than functions in your business?	☐	☐
• Is it clear what the strategic business processes are and how well they perform?	☐	☐
• Are your key processes being systematically slimmed and/or re-engineered and are your non-key processes being removed?	☐	☐
• Is your process management multiplying (rather than adding) value?	☐	☐
• Overall, is your business lean and responsive?	☐	☐

People: harnessing talent and pride	**Yes**	**No**
• Is teamwork natural and flexible throughout the organisation?	☐	☐
• Do you have a continuous flow of people's ideas and are you using them?	☐	☐
• Is your business one big community in which people help each other out?	☐	☐
• Are your people continually developed for their roles in the business?	☐	☐
• Do they feel valued?	☐	☐

Disciplines: achieving structured, coordinated action	**Yes**	**No**
• Do people know the cost of waste and the value of good work across the business?	☐	☐
• Do people work to agreed procedures and make improvements and changes in a methodical, ordered way?	☐	☐
• Do people, including managers (that means you too), use improvement tools?	☐	☐
• Do your people work to standards? Could they say what being professional in their work means?	☐	☐
• Can you see multi-level improvement disciplines being applied simultaneously in the business and are you orchestrating their combined effect?	☐	☐

Integration: pulling it all together to accelerate improvement **Yes** **No**

- Do you manage the change process through a pro-active implementation strategy, communicated in an explicit improvement plan? ☐ ☐
- Have you learned from others' experiences and are these lessons built into the plan? ☐ ☐
- Are you using all the key interventions (workshops, surveys, events, training, ommunications, displays, disciplines, tools, recognition, etc) and integrating them into a coherent process? ☐ ☐
- Are you managing the dynamics of change through the line? ☐ ☐
- Is the rate of improvement increasing?

Results: making improvement pay **Yes** **No**

- Have you set and communicated specific expectations of multiple benefits? ☐ ☐
- Are you managing for short-term benefits as well as long-term success? ☐ ☐
- Are people outside interested in what you are doing... is it showing? ☐ ☐
- Is the improvement process self-financing and handsomely so? ☐ ☐
- Is your business demonstrably better than eighteen months ago? ☐ ☐

2. **Score your responses**

There are 50 questions.

How many negatives did you record?

Under 5:

- you must be applying most of the tools in this Toolbox already, well done!

Under 12:

- some fine tuning required, but your approach to change is in reasonably good shape.

Between 13 and 25:

- if your change programme is less than two years old, the next year is going to be tough.
- if more than two years old, you're not getting the most benefit from it.

Over 25:

- you really need to use this Toolbox!

Chart your YES answers on the diagram opposite to give a visual picture of where you are now.

How often did you say YES?

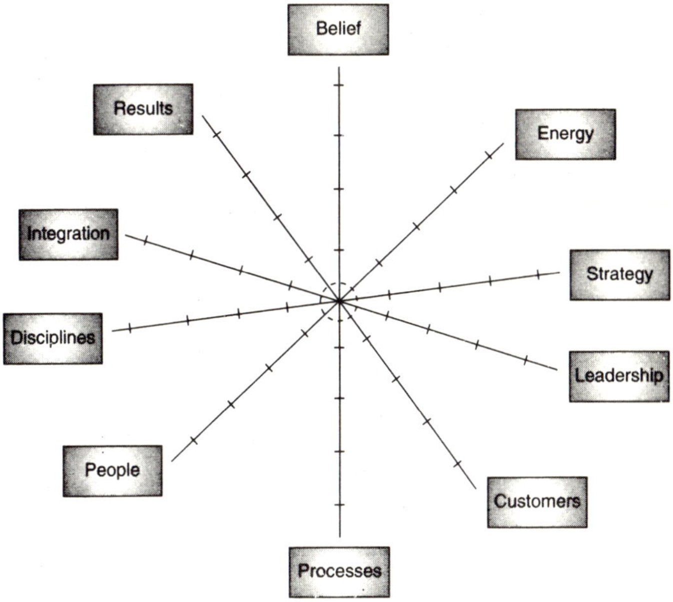

3. Decide which areas you need to work on and refer to the relevant section(s) in this Toolbox for ideas on where to start.

How it helps

It is important to be realistic about your organisation's fitness for change. This tool gives a quick and simple method of diagnosis against the Quest model for transforming your business.

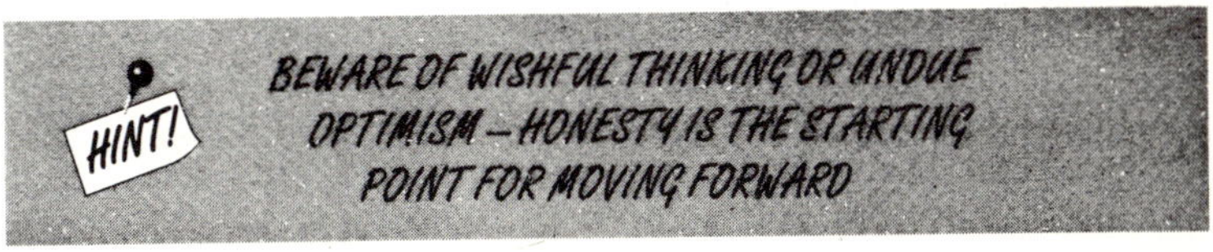

Implement Change

What it is

Once the need and direction for change are established, you can go on to plan how to achieve it in a way that will allow you to tackle the eight drivers.

Quest has developed a four stage implementation process which has proved highly successful in transforming organisations.

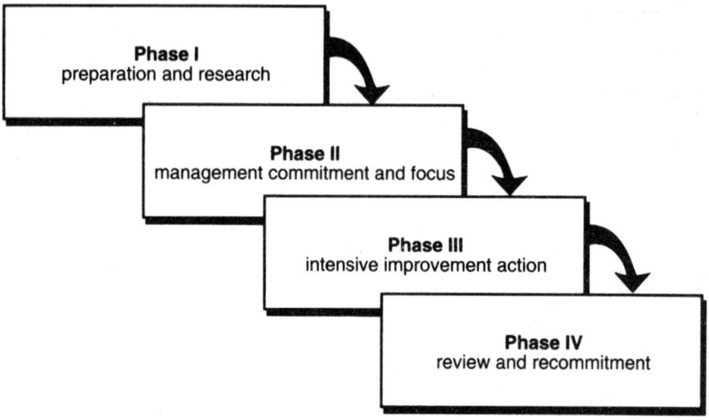

How to use it

Phase 1 – preparation and research

1. Decide what preparation and research is needed. For example:
   - Customer survey?
   - Employee survey?
   - Process analysis?
   - Resource audit?
2. Agree how you will share the results of your research:
   - Written report?
   - Presentation(s)?

- Displays?

Who needs to know?

3. Agree who is going to coordinate the change process and who will be involved/affected:

- How will you involve them/inform them of your plans?
- Do you need to appoint formal 'facilitators' to support the change process?

Phase II – management commitment and focus

4. Plan how you will ensure management commitment and focus:

- Who needs to be involved?
- Do you need to brief and/or train?
- How can you turn commitment into action?
- How will you avoid overload?

Phase III – intensive improvement action

5. Plan how you will get everyone else involved:

- Understanding the strategy
- Trained to use tools and techniques
- Focusing on customers and processes
- Energised and committed to change
- Improving their everyday work in a systematic and effective way.

6. Agree how you will measure progress. By:

- Level of involvement?
- Use of tools and techniques?
- Improved performance?
- Role model behaviours?

Phase IV – review and recommit

7. Decide at what point you will formally review progress and recommit to further change:

- Who will be involved?
- Will you need to re-survey?
- How will you keep things 'fresh'?

How it helps

This four stage approach to implementation gives a systematic and structured approach to change which ensures everyone is involved; effort is focused on results and progress is measured and reviewed.

HINT!

PLAN WHAT YOU'RE GOING TO DO;
DO IT AND THEN REVIEW HOW YOU'VE DONE IT;
THEN DO SOME MORE!

2 Start with belief

Have a Vision

What it is

A vision has four components. There are, therefore, four main activities involved in developing a vision. This tool outlines each of the components and suggests a process for developing them.

How to use it

Review the definitions of each of the four components and use the tips within each to help develop a vision for your whole organisation, department or team.

1. Clarify your purpose

The 'purpose' of an organisation is a succinct statement of the 'core reason' for its existence. It defines what it does as well as what it does not do.

The key questions that you need to ask in determining your purpose are:

- why do we exist as an organisation?
- what is our primary and overriding objective?

Examples of purpose statements:

Philips Petroleum define their purpose as

"... to enhance the value of our shareholders' investment".

Ford's purpose is:

"... to be a low cost producer of the highest quality products and services which provide the best customer value".

Colworth Laboratories' purpose is:

"... to be first with new ideas which provide competitive advantage from science and technology".

At a business unit or departmental level the same requirement for clarity of purpose exists.

Ask yourself:

- where does your 'team' fit within the larger organisation?
- why does your 'team' exist?
- what is your purpose statement?

2. Define your values

Another element of the big picture is what we stand for or what we value. Values express the influences behind how people will behave in order to achieve their purpose and what they believe in.

Values therefore reflect the style and behaviour of the organisation, for example:

> **The CO-OPERATIVE BANK**
>
> We, The Co-operative Bank Group, will continue to develop a successful and innovative financial institution by providing our customers with high-quality financial and related services whilst promoting the underlying principles of co-operation which are:
>
> **Quality and Excellence** to offer all our customers consistent high-quality and good value services and strive for excellence in all that we do.
>
> **Participation** to introduce and promote the concept of full participation to all our customers and staff.
>
> **Retentions** to manage the business effectively and efficiently, attracting investment and maintaining sufficient surplus funds within the business to ensure continued development of the Group.
>
> **Education and Training** to act as a caring and responsible employer encouraging the development and training of all our staff and encourage commitment and pride in each other and the Group.
>
> **Co-operation** to develop a close affinity with organisations which promote fellowship between workers, customers, members and employers.
>
> **Quality of Life** to be a responsible member of society by promoting an environment where the needs of local communities can be met now and in the future.
>
> **Freedom** of association to be non-partisan in all social, political, racial and religious matters.
>
> **Integrity** to act at all times with honesty and integrity and within legislative and regulatory requirements.
>
> ***Statement of Values at the Co-operative Bank***

However, statements of values can cause confusion and leave people either feeling uncertain about the way they should behave or noting inconsistencies with current behaviours.

It is therefore helpful to articulate the behaviours that will bring the values to life. An example is given on the next page.

We value openness and honesty as a basis for establishing effective relationships with others and as an essential part of a culture which encourages all to freely express their ideas and views.

We would expect this to be reflected in behaviour which:

- does not hide information except that which is, of necessity, confidential
- provides the facts as they are
- keeps people informed/acts as a regular and reliable source of information
- expresses our values and gives feedback in a positive and open style
- encourages active listening
- leads to consultations before decisions and action
- supports management by trust, not interference
- leads by example

What you can do:

- If you do not have stated values in your organisation, use the following chart to identify what appears to be valued now and how this might need to change in the future
- Select the five most important values that you feel will contribute to the future success of your organisation
- Describe the behaviours you would expect to see for each of these

What do you really value?

Which of the following are the most important contributors to the long-term success of your business? It might help to think both of those factors which you value now and those on which you should put more value to ensure future prosperity...

Values	Now	Future
• Customer loyalty		
• Long-term return		
• Short-term return		
• Market share		
• Beating the competition		
• Profitability		
• Information		
• External image		
• Technology		
• Productivity		
• Innovation		
• Synergy between units		
• Being the best		
• Balancing the budget		
• Return on shareholder investment		
• Improving society		
• Protecting the environment		
• Helping the local community		
• Speed		
• Cost reduction		
• Flexibility		
• Managing suppliers		
• Our products		
• Our people		
• The management team		
• Trust		
• Integrity		
• Value for money		
• Distinctive products		
• Superior products		
• Others...		

- Ensure that those you would expect to 'live the values' understand, agree and accept them, are able to practise them – and will be recognised for practising them.

3. Describe your culture

Culture is how you do things. There is already a culture in your organisation, whether it is articulated or not. It is the way you tend to respond and react... the way you do things. But it may well not be very consistent with the achievement of your organisation's vision of its future. In which case, what would be your ideal way of operating?

Defining a cultural vision not only gives direction but also early pointers to some of the wider barriers to be overcome. For instance:

- If you know your vision is of self-managed workteams, then what do you do about the current layers of supervision and how will local managers relate to the newly-enfranchised teams?
- If you intend to move over to process management and make your top executives responsible for processes, how do you maintain centres of functional excellence such as buying, accounting, planning?
- What about the grading and appraisal systems – how will they need to change?

These issues should be thought through and the necessary changes planned in advance.

- What are the main cultural features of your organisation? Use the chart on the next page to help your diagnosis.
- Which three features will need the most work? Where will you start?

Cultural features of your organisation/team		
	Now	How it needs to be
• Self-managed teams • Continuous improvement of processes • Customer-driven behaviours (service mentality) • Partnership relationships (with customers, suppliers and third parties) • Waste reduction (excessive or misaligned time and cost removed) • Minimal hierarchy • One status only • Performance-related rewards • Data driven (relevant information at the right place and time) • Internal market (with customer/supplier contracts) • Internal networks and temporary, issue-focused teams • Empowered workforce • High energy • Learning, developing environment • Innovative, challenging environment • Continuous, constructive feedback • Disciplined focused action • Postitive communication flow • Measured, benchmarked activity • Pride with humility • Others...		

4. Develop your mission

A mission is the link between vision and strategy. A mission converts the vision into what has to be done to get there. (In turn, breakthrough goals specify what must be done this year to make progress towards the mission.) A mission statement is usually descriptive and is often used to communicate the components of the vision to a wider audience in such a way that excites and challenges individuals.

- What is the mission statement of your organisation?
- Is it:
  - clear?
  - compelling?
  - long term?
  - meaningful to others?
  - succinct?
- How can it be improved?
- If you don't already have a mission statement, reflect on the notes you made for purpose, values and culture and draft one.

Examples of mission statements:

Pullman Food's mission statement

- To satisfy our customers
- To value and develop our people
- Thereby to make more profit

Boeing's mission statement

To remain the world's foremost aerospace company through the innovative design, development, production, marketing and support of high quality, cost-competitive products and services while:

- providing strong financial performance for stockholders
- maintaining the highest standards of integrity, and
- recognising and rewarding employee achievements

Ford's mission statement

- To improve, continually, our products and services to meet our customers' needs, allowing us to prosper as a business and to provide a reasonable return for our stockholders, the owners of our business.

How it helps

A vision is crucial in giving a sense of direction and purpose to a team or organisation. As long as it is followed through into detailed plans and actions it will energise and enthuse those involved. This tool defines the elements of a meaningful vision and poses questions to help you develop your own. By going through this process you will be testing whether or not you really have the belief and hunger to implement successful and (if necessary) radical change.

3 Develop a strategy – know where you're going

Use Scenario Planning

What it is

As the world becomes more turbulent and the rate of change increases, it is getting harder and harder to predict and therefore to plan for the future. It is no longer enough to assume the future will be a continuation of the past.

Scenario planning is a tool to help you reflect on alternative futures as a step towards setting the most robust strategy possible.

How to use it

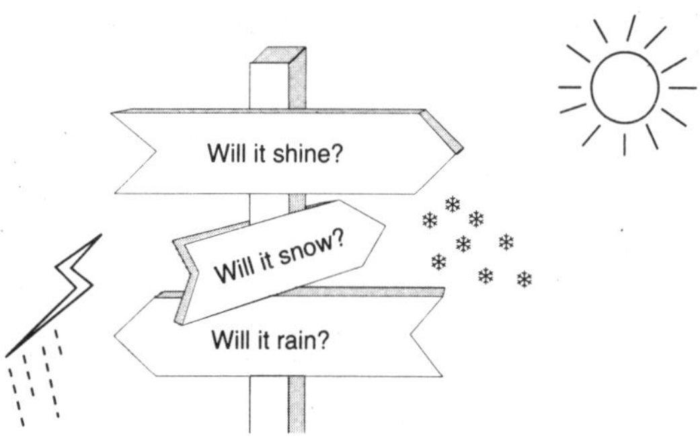

1. Decide on what scale you are planning:

- Global?
- National?
- Local?
- Whole company?
- Specific team?
- Next month/year/decade/century?

2. Try and forget your past. Put aside all your assumptions about past success/trends/patterns, etc. (This is very hard to do but it's important to avoid the blinkers that the past can give you.)

3. Brainstorm all of the external things that influence your business and group them under headings. You will probably find categories like:

4. To keep it simple initially, agree which three of these external factors have the most impact on your business.

5. For each factor identify likely options for the future, eg raw materials:

   - The price of crude oil doubles in two years.
   - Cheap wheat is no longer available from America.
   - There is a glut of silicon chips.

6. Combine the possibilities into three or four different scenarios. See examples of scenarios on next page.

Scenario 1	*Scenario 2*
(a shower manufacturer)	(a food distributor)
– a new government is elected and interest rates increase by 5%.	– the recession ends and consumer spending increases rapidly.
– the long, hot summers continue and water is rationed.	– restrictions on irradiating food are removed.
– a new tax is introduced on road haulage.	– the 'green' lobby leads to local authority targets for 50% recycling of all packaging.

7. Ensure that your scenarios 'hang together' and are credible.

8. Turn each scenario into a reasonably detailed narrative with sufficient detail to be 'real'.

9. Take each scenario in turn (this can be done by separate teams).

- Really try and 'think yourself' into the scenario. Let it be real.
- Identify what you would need to do as a business to survive and prosper in these circumstances.
- Start by brainstorming (to avoid your assumptions and prejudices limiting your ideas).
- Think through the implications for all your stakeholders – customers, employees, suppliers, etc.
- Develop your thoughts into specific strategies.

10. Review your work.

- Are there any strategies common to all scenarios? If so, these would seem a good starting point.
- Are there any strategies that might work in one scenario but be very damaging in another? These are high risk.
- Are there any strategies that could be adapted or developed depending on how things happen in practice? These have less risk.

11. Decide on the strategies you wish to adopt to move forward into the future. Use these as a starting point for defining your breakthrough goals.

12. Identify ways of tracking your external world so that you will know quickly if the scenario is changing and you can adapt your strategy.

What it is

Scenario planning is a technique for identifying options for the future. It should be used at the very beginning of the planning process. It will help you to avoid falling into the trap of assuming tomorrow will be like yesterday.

HINT!

DON'T ASSUME THE FUTURE WILL BE LIKE THE PAST

Focus on Balanced Breakthroughs

What it is

There is a danger of taking a one-dimensional view when planning corporate change. This tool will help you to take a balanced view and establish goals covering all the vital aspects of your business, namely:

- Markets.
- Operations.
- Culture.
- Finance.

How to use it

1. Review the four goal areas:

Markets:

- Are you clear what you are trying to achieve for your customers in terms of product, service or price?
- Do you have goals for market share or position?
- Are you trying to break into new markets?

Operations:

- Are you clear what your major processes are?
- Are you focused on improving these processes in terms of cycle times, waste reduction or productivity?
- Are you using the most appropriate systems and technology?

Culture:

- Does your organisation strive to meet the needs of all of your stakeholders (customers, suppliers, employees, shareholders and local community)?
- Do you put effort into developing your people?
- Have you built a culture of continuous improvement?

Finance:

- Are you clear what ultimately you have to achieve in terms of sales, profits and returns?
- Is your borrowing under control?

2. Complete a table of your existing goals in the 4 areas:

Goal area	What you aim to achieve	By how much?	By when?
Markets			
Operations			
Culture			
Finance			

3. Now review the table:

- Are you trying to do too much and achieving too little?
- Are there large gaps where you have no goals or targets?
- Do you have something in all 4 areas or are you just focused on finance?
- Are your goals stretching (100% plus improvement) or all in small steps?
- Do your goals really have impact on what you do or how you run your business?

4. If you are DISSATISFIED with your existing goals then:

- brainstorm all your options
- identify the 2/3 most important goals in each area (the 'vital few')
- set yourself stretching targets – BE BOLD!
- summarise your output and present it to your team for discussion and comment
- once you have all accepted what your goals are, you are ready to consider how to achieve them.

How it helps

Focusing on balanced breakthroughs is a tool to help you consider all of the important areas of your business when planning the future. It will help you to develop a stretching, but realistic, range of goals to strive for.

> **HINT!** IT'S BETTER TO HAVE A FEW FIRES WHICH BURN BRIGHTLY RATHER THAN LOTS THAT ONLY GENTLY SMOULDER

Be SMART

What it is

Goals give a team something to aim at which can be quite broad and can be achieved in a variety of ways.

Goals are general statements of purpose and direction. They are usually short, simple statements summarising what is to be changed and in what direction. For example: to increase profitability; to remove differentials; to open new branches; to improve service.

Objectives are very clear statements of what output you need to achieve, eg 'To reduce paper waste by 50% by year end'.

Effective objectives are more comprehensive than goals and should be **SMART:**

Specific: express objectives in terms of the specific results you want to achieve, not in terms of the activities needed to achieve them, ie outputs not inputs. Avoid ambiguity.

Measurable: identify what measures you will use to judge success. Make them as quantifiable and specific as possible, eg time/quantity/quality/cost. Use customer-related as well as internal measures.

Agreed: an individual or team should have the opportunity to discuss and buy in to the objective rather than simply have it imposed.

Realistic: neither too easy so that talents are underused, nor too difficult so that the individual or team burns itself out. Take past performance into account in assessing realism. Be sure the objective is realistic given the resource available and the demands of other priorities.

Timebound: include a date by which the objective should be achieved and also interim milestones and review points if the overall timescale is long. Choose an appropriate timeframe given the level and complexity of the team and task.

This tool outlines how to go about agreeing effective objectives.

How to use it

1. Identify/agree your goals.
2. If you already have objectives, are they SMART?
3. If not, how can you improve them using these guidelines?
4. Agree the priorities between your objectives with your boss/team.
5. Collate all of this information onto a chart:

Goals	Objectives			Priority
	What	How much	By when	

6. Use your chart regularly to check and review your progress.
7. A typical process for agreeing and tracking goals and objectives which need project team(s) to achieve them is shown on the following page:

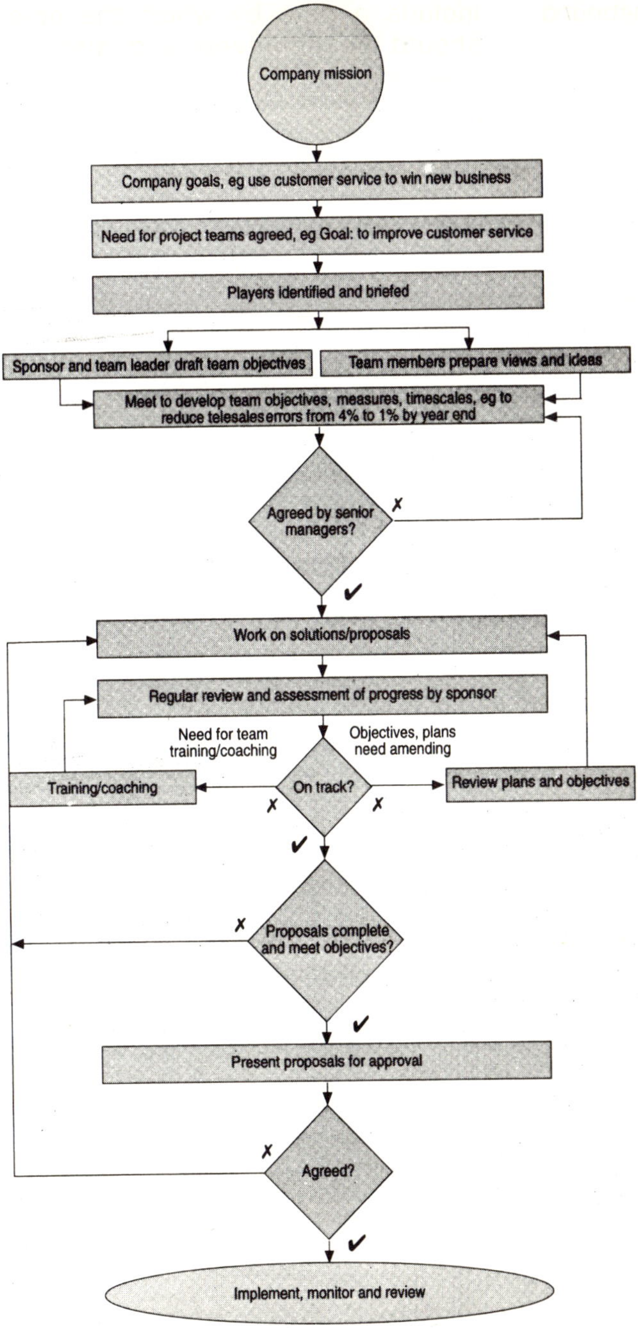
Company mission
Company goals, eg use customer service to win new business
Need for project teams agreed, eg Goal: to improve customer service
Players identified and briefed
Sponsor and team leader draft team objectives
Team members prepare views and ideas
Meet to develop team objectives, measures, timescales, eg to reduce telesales errors from 4% to 1% by year end
Agreed by senior managers?
Work on solutions/proposals
Regular review and assessment of progress by sponsor
Need for team training/coaching
Objectives, plans need amending
Training/coaching
On track?
Review plans and objectives
Proposals complete and meet objectives?
Present proposals for approval
Agreed?
Implement, monitor and review

HINT! EFFECTIVE OBJECTIVES ALLOW SUCCESS; BEWARE OF BUILDING IN FAILURE

How it helps

Establishing useful goals and objectives takes time, effort and skill. The benefits of doing it, however, far outweigh the difficulties.

Establishing goals and objectives will help you to:

- ensure the team's work is relevant and adds value
- have more control over resources and actions
- know what people are working on
- coordinate individual efforts
- have an overall picture of progress
- assess performance (team and individual)
- identify problems early
- look ahead and anticipate change
- improve communication in your team.

It also helps individuals because each will have:

- direction, clear expectations and defined boundaries
- more freedom to get on with the job
- means for receiving feedback
- a way of identifying training and development needs.

HINT! GOALS GIVE A SENSE OF PURPOSE AND DIRECTION, SPECIFIC OBJECTIVES GIVE PERFORMANCE MEASURES

Cascade Your Goals Using Catchball

What it is

Catchball is an iterative technique for getting buy in to goals and developing plans for achieving them.

How to use it

1. Define your mission, values and culture.
2. Develop your breakthrough goals.
3. Communicate your goals through your normal line (use team briefing if this is in place).
4. Ask your immediate reports to develop proposals on how they will tackle each goal. Ask them to draft a planning table outlining the targets, owners and timescales.
5. Meet to discuss their proposals. Check that they:
   - have considered alternatives
   - are being stretching yet realistic
   - have thought through the implications.
6. Once you are all in agreement at this level, ask them to repeat the process with their direct reports, developing in more detail how they will achieve the goals.
7. If necessary, repeat the process through another level to ensure the plans are in sufficient detail to identify specific tasks/improvement projects.

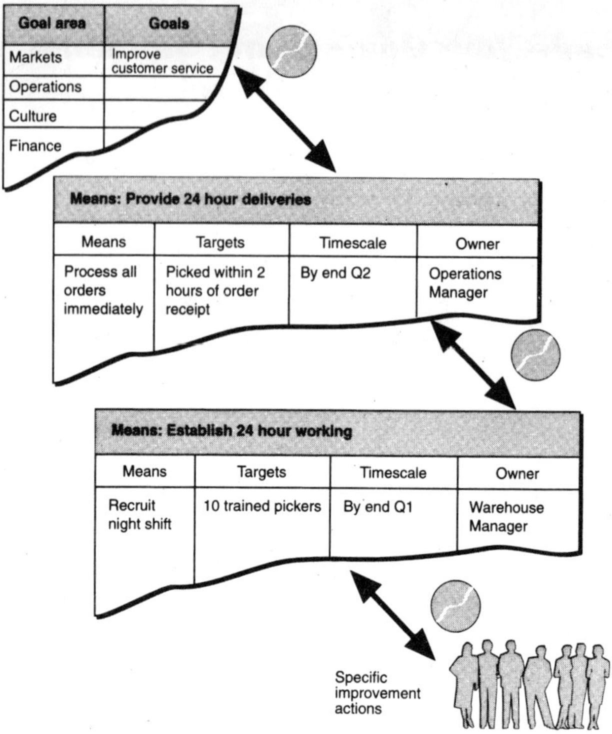

8. Once all of the planning tables are drafted, reverse the process, ie confirm and finalise the detailed plans, which in turn provides evidence that the higher level plans are realistic which in turn ensures the initial means and targets can be satisfied. If at any point changes need to be made the catchball should move up or down the line until there is consensus on what needs to be done.

How it helps

Catchball is a practical tool for ensuring that improvement actions are ultimately tied in to the breakthrough goals by a series of cascaded and debated planning tables. This ensures involvement by everyone at the appropriate level, so increasing their commitment and ensuring agreed, planned and focused action.

4 Lead the way – be an effective change agent

Be a Role Model

What it is

If others are to take you seriously and implement change at your instigation, you must behave in a way which builds their respect and commitment. This tool outlines the key behaviours of a change agent under the headings of:

- Being customer focused.
- Challenging the status quo.
- Promoting tough standards.
- Being visible and available.
- Championing excellence.
- Acting with integrity.
- Teamworking.

The behaviours are in questionnaire format so that you can assess yourself and also use it as a framework to seek feedback from others.

How to use it

1. There are ten questions on each element. For each question, rate yourself on a scale from 1 to 6:

   1 Very poor; in need of significant improvement.

   2 Poor; needs some work.

   3 Some problems here; though not too bad.

   4 OK; but could be better.

   5 Good; improvements would be marginal.

   6 Very good; no need to focus improvement here.

You could also gain valuable feedback by asking others to complete the questionnaire about you.

Section 1: Being customer focused

I am clear who my immediate customers are	☐
I regularly spend time agreeing requirements with my customers	☐
I regularly receive feedback from my customers	☐
I encourage feedback from my customers	☐
I regularly take action to improve the standard of per my personal outputs to delight my customers	☐
I encourage feedback on my actions and behaviour from others	☐
My area spends time agreeing requirements with customers	☐
My area has clear measures of customer satisfaction	☐
I do not allow departmentalism/blinkered attitudes to colour decisions that affect customers	☐
I use customer satisfaction as a key measure in all my decisions	☐
Total	
Average score (divide total by 10)	☐

What are your priorities for improvement in this area?

Section 2: Challenging the status quo

- [ ] I do not tolerate poor standards in any circumstances
- [ ] I continually question the way things are done as a way of stimulating improvement
- [ ] I am receptive to and welcome new ideas
- [ ] I invest my time and resources in improvement activity
- [ ] I allow my people to experiment, make changes and take risks
- [ ] I encourage others to question and challenge the status quo
- [ ] I do say 'no' and explain why
- [ ] People feel free to express their views to me
- [ ] My area has clear improvement goals that are monitored regularly
- [ ] Everyone in my team has at least one improvement goal towards which they are working

Total

Average score (divide total by 10) ☐

What are your priorities for improvement in this area?

Section 3: Promoting challenging standards

- [ ] I have measures that tell me how I am doing
- [ ] I use data to make decisions wherever possible
- I insist that outputs from my area match customer requirements
- [ ] I put effort into preventing rather than correcting errors
- [ ] I delegate authority and set challenging targets for others to achieve
- [ ] I set clear expectations on the standards I want
- [ ] I always set or agree demanding improvement goals for myself

I coach my team to adopt high personal standards and behaviours ☐
I censure anyone who deliberately compromises agreed performance standards ☐
I spend time planning the personal development of my staff ☐
Total
Average score (divide total by 10)
What are your priorities for improvement in this area? ☐

Section 4: Being visible and available

I regularly walk about in my area ☐
I spend time with people at their place of work ☐
I encourage people to approach me when they need to ☐
I am able to pick up early warning signals of problems ☐
I listen to the views and ideas of my team ☐
I am accessible, people can see me when they need to ☐
I maintain good relationships and internal contacts ☐
I regularly talk to staff ☐
I know what is important to my people ☐
I look for examples of excellent behaviour and actions in others ☐
Total
Average score (divide total by 10)
What are your priorities for improvement in this area? ☐

Section 5: Championing excellence

I invest in activities to improve performance ☐
I apply the principle of Plan-Do-Check-Act (PDCA) in my daily work ☐
I use problem-solving tools whenever possible ☐
I hold regular meetings with my staff to stimulate improvement activity ☐
I talk about our mission and improvement goals ☐
I encourage continuous improvement through my own behaviours ☐
I fully recognise high standards of performance ☐
I am open about my mistakes and learn from them ☐
I am always punctual and well prepared ☐
I treat errors as opportunities for improvement ☐

Total

Average score (divide total by 10) ☐

What are your priorities for improvement in this area?

- -

- -

Section 6: Acting with integrity

I treat others with fairness, trust and respect ☐
I never feed the grapevine by gossiping ☐
I always keep my promises ☐
I hit deadlines which I have agreed ☐
I only give feedback constructively, not destructively ☐
I am always honest with others ☐
I fight hard for what I believe in ☐
My actions reflect what I say ☐
I explain the reasons for decisions ☐
I set clear priorities and maintain consistent direction ☐

Total

Average score (divide total by 10)

What are your priorities for improvement in this area? ☐

Section 7: Teamworking

- I seek all views and give everyone their say ☐
- My direct reports work with me as a team ☐
- I respect and work together with my peers ☐
- I am perceived as decisive but not as autocratic ☐
- I do not obstruct collective decisions once made ☐
- I listen generously with an open mind ☐
- I agree clear goals, targets and standards with my team ☐
- I invest time developing my team to work more effectively together ☐
- I ensure everyone has the knowledge and skills they need to play their part ☐
- I encourage my team regularly to review our performance ☐

Total

Average score (divide total by 10)

What are your priorities for improvement in this area? ☐

----

2. Transfer your average score for each section on to the spider diagram on the next page. If you have asked others to complete the questionnaire on you, add their average scores to the diagram and look for the gaps. Ask yourself why these gaps (if any) exist and how you can explore them further.

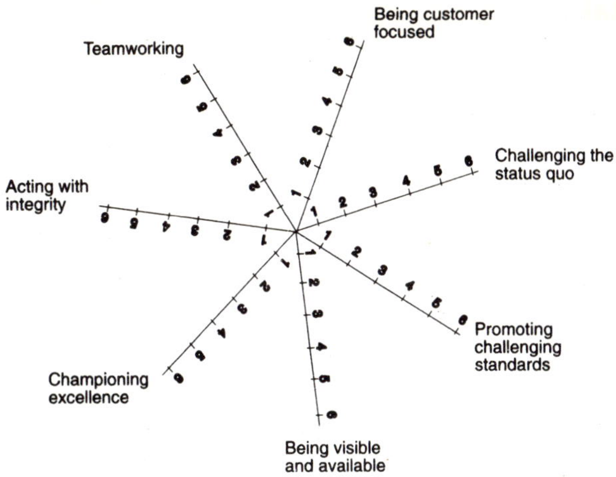

Your views

Others' views

Scale
1 very poor, in need of significant improvement
2 poor, needs some work
3 some problems here, though not too bad
4 OK, but could be better
5 good, improvements would be marginal
6 very good, no need to focus improvement here

3. When you have completed all the sections, review your chosen priorities and identify three areas to work on over the next six months. It is acceptable to choose more than one area from a particular section if this best reflects your needs.

	Behaviour to improve	Actions I intend to take	When
1.			
2.			
3.			

How it helps

This tool helps you to identify the specific leadership behaviours that you need to work on to become a better change agent.

Recognise Success

What it is

The way in which people work is strongly influenced by the way leaders react. When working under pressure, it is easy to react only negatively when there are problems or poor results. However, if you want people to try new ways to experiment or take risks in order to improve performance, you must respond positively and constructively to their efforts as well as to their results.

There are many ways in which recognition can be shown, both formal and informal.

This tool outlines a range of approaches to recognition for you to review and from which you can select.

How to use it

The following elements have all been incorporated successfully into formal recognition schemes by different companies:

- **Goals, measures, standards and targets**

  Unless performance is related back to the goals of the company/team/individual, there is no objective way of assessing whether recognition is appropriate.

  Crosfield (a UK chemical company) formally assess every OFI (Opportunity for Improvement) against the contribution to company goals and provide a range of responses.

- **Training and development**

  While basic training to do a job should be provided for everyone, attendance and achievement in training can be a useful form of recognition (certificates and presentations). Development through involvement in projects, visits, new tasks, deputising, etc is an ideal way of recognising earlier efforts.

- **Everyday behaviour**

  Formal recognition will seem hollow and meaningless if not supported by day-to-day actions and behaviours. Informal, spontaneous recognition involves:

  – listening to ideas, suggestions, problems
  – encouraging and supporting involvement in improvement activities
  – being visible, accessible and approachable
  – having positive expectations about individuals' ability and potential
  – understanding each individual's motivation needs and providing appropriate recognition for them
  – most of all giving praise and thanks for efforts, results and appropriate behaviour.

1. Review the various approaches to recognition. Which do you think would work for you?
2. Where will you start?
3. How will you go about it?
4. How will you ensure you are fair and consistent?

HINT! *RECOGNITION FEEDS FUTURE PERFORMANCE*

How it helps

This tool identifies a range of approaches to recognition (both formal and informal) to help you select those best for your organisation.

Live with Ambiguity

What it is

Change means uncertainty. It can involve letting go of the familiar before a new routine is established. An ability to cope with ambiguity is therefore a useful asset for surviving in a changing world.

This tool uses a questionnaire, developed by Adrian Furnham, to assess how likely we are to see change and ambiguity as a positive opportunity rather than as a jungle full of danger.

How to use it

1. Complete the questionnaire and calculate your score

Do you think each of the statements below is true or false? Tick the appropriate box:

	True	False
a. An expert who doesn't come up with a definite answer probably doesn't know a great deal	☐	☐
b. A good job is one where what is to be done and how it is to be done are clearly specified	☐	☐
c. In the long run it is possible to get more done by tackling small, simple problems rather than larger, complicated ones	☐	☐
d. A person who leads an even, regular life in which few surprises or unexpected happenings arise has a lot to be grateful for	☐	☐

	True	False
e. I like parties where I know most of the people more than ones where all or most are complete strangers	☐	☐
f. The sooner we all acquire similar values and ideas the better	☐	☐
g. People who schedule their lives all the time probably miss most of the joy of living	☐	☐
h. It is more fun to tackle a complicated problem than to solve a simple one	☐	☐
i. People who insist on a yes or no answer don't know how complicated things really are	☐	☐
j. Many of our most important decisions are based on insufficient information	☐	☐
k. Managers who hand out vague assignments give a chance for subordinates to show initiative and originality	☐	☐
l. I have always felt that there is a clear difference between right and wrong	☐	☐
m. Nothing gets accomplished unless you stick to some basic rules	☐	☐
n. Vague and impressionistic pictures really have little appeal for me	☐	☐

	True	False
o. Before an examination, I feel less anxious if I know how many questions there will be	☐	☐
p. Sometimes I enjoy going against the rules and doing things I'm not supposed to	☐	☐
q. I like to fool around with new ideas, even if they turn out to be a waste of time	☐	☐
r. If I were a doctor, I would prefer the uncertainties of a psychiatrist to the clear and definite work of a surgeon	☐	☐
s. I don't like to work on a problem unless there is a possibility of an unambiguous answer	☐	☐
t. It bothers me when I am unable to follow another person's train of thought	☐	☐

2. Score your responses:

The higher the score the more intolerant of ambiguity you are. Score one for each *True* response for questions a–f, k–o and t. Score one for each *False* response for questions g–j and p–s.

Score 0-8: Perhaps an arty, creative type.

Score 9-15: A pretty normal score. You are happy to recognise and deal with life's little uncertainties.

Score 16-20: A conservative, call-a-spade-a-spade, see things in black and white type.

3. Decide what to do

If you have scored low, you probably don't need to focus on improving your tolerance of ambiguity!

If you have a high score, you probably need to work on this area. The following checklist gives some practical ideas on what you can do.

- ✔ Push yourself to try out new experiences rather than sticking to familiar activities
- ✔ Get involved in activities that will force you to meet new people. Talk to them to find out their views and ideas
- ✔ Take on a new project which is large/complicated/ vague and which you are unclear how to tackle
- ✔ Practise seeing both sides of a debate/the pros and cons/strengths and weaknesses/pluses and minuses
- ✔ Say "If I were...I would..." and work out what you would say or do if you were really in their shoes
- ✔ Examine all alternatives to solving a problem or achieving a result, not just the most familiar. Try something new for the sake of it
- ✔ Say words like "I don't know"/"I'm not sure" and see how others react – it won't be as bad as you think
- ✔ Delay making decisions until the facts are clear and the options highlighted
- ✔ Ask questions rather than give answers when people come to you with problems. Help them to find their own solutions
- ✔ Above all, don't worry...it's a waste of energy!

How it helps

An ability to live with ambiguity makes it easier not just to cope with change but to instigate and proactively make change happen. This tool helps you assess your style in this area and gives some practical tips on how to improve.

5 Focus on your customers

Think Customer; Act Customer

What it is

his tool will help you to assess your current approach to your customers. By answering a series of questions you can test whether or not you really THINK CUSTOMER; ACT CUSTOMER.

How to use it

1. Review the following questions to assess your current approach to customers (both internal and external).

- **Who is your customer?** Identify your markets and focus on the people you deliver to, both inside and outside of your organisation. Aim to concentrate on one person – your customer – at a time. Cut down a mass market into segments and use one customer as a model for each market category.
- **Have you allocated time for your customer?** Believe that your customers are your business and therefore divide your week up so that you see them.
- **Do you understand their needs?** Observe and listen. Immerse yourself in their environment. Watch your customers.
- **Have you pinned down their immediate requirements and agreed them?** Don't make assumptions, test that your interpretation is correct by asking them to confirm.

- **Have you built feedback mechanisms?** Enable your customer to tell you easily how you are doing. Run surveys, open and blind, to check the accuracy of this channel.
- **Are you smoothing the interface?** Continually make it easy for your customer to do business with you. Look at your customer's experience of dealing with you as a whole, from initial enquiry through development to billing; identify and remove any barriers, even if this makes life harder inside the organisation.
- **Have you built in flexibility?** Expect your customers to have needs way outside of the agreed parameters and be prepared to help by having the capacity to adjust.
- **Are you serving, not selling?** Be attentive and courteous; indifference or arrogance is heaviiy penalised. Your customer is your partner; don't short-change him.
- **Are you looking for trends and anticipating emerging needs?** Accumulate data on your customers and look for patterns. Look around all the influences on them – competitors (yours and theirs), regulatory bodies, community, consumer taste – and imagine how any potential changes would affect your customers and their needs. Be just ahead of the game; don't raise expectations youcannot sustain.
- **Can you do something special?** Periodically, go out of your way to do something extra for your customers. A delighted customer is your best salesman.

2. Which of these 10 areas do you most need to work on?

3. How can you go about it? – refer to other, more specific tools to help you.

How it helps

You will only take action if you accept the need for change. This tool will help yuou to assess how much you need to improve your approach to your customers.

Establish Customer-Supplier Agreements

What it is

A Customer-Supplier Agreement (CSA) is a written document detailing:

- the needs of a customer (either internal or external)
- what the supplier can deliver
- what is to be done to improve the delivery of the customer requirements.

It is sometimes called a 'service level agreement'.

How to use it

1. Decide on the customer-supplier relationship to be addressed

The two main players – the supplier of the output and the customer – should agree in principle that a CSA would improve their working relationship.

2. Identify other interested parties

Make sure that all interested parties understand what is happening and are willing to 'buy in' to the CSA.

3. Prepare for the meeting

The two main players should individually review their customer-supplier relationship to generate ideas on needs and improvement targets. Data can also be gathered to make the discussion more objective.

The following CSA checklist will help you prepare:

Agreement checklist

- ✔ Who are the customer and supplier?
- ✔ Are there other interested parties?
- ✔ What are the customer requirements?
- ✔ How are the outputs to be measured?
- ✔ How is customer feedback to be monitored?
- ✔ What are the respective responsibilities and actions of the customer and supplier to ensure the agreed output?

Other headings, (eg what to do in case of disagreement) may be added as appropriate.

4. CSA discussion

The main players (and other interested parties if appropriate) should meet to discuss and develop an agreement.

Aim to keep the draft as simple as possible. A pro forma is shown on the next page along with instructions on what to put in each box.

5. Trial period

The initial agreement should be for a trial period and amended as required at the end of this time.

6. Regular review

The CSA should then be reviewed on a regular basis by the main players in order to update needs and performance measures and identify actions to further improve the relationship.

CUSTOMER-SUPPLIER AGREEMENT: Pro forma

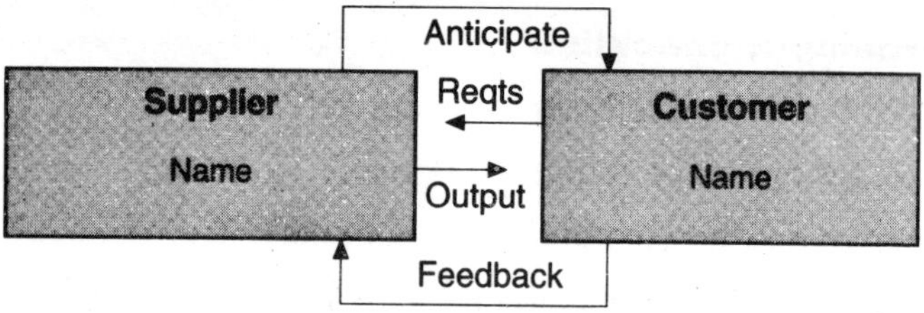

Supplier specification

Detailed standards, inputs and feedback the supplier needs to meet the customer's requirements

Customer requirements

What outputs the customer needs (these can be negotiated)

Measures Units of progress by which the supplier and customer will know if the needs are being met to the required standards	**Actual** Current performance	**Target** Required performance

Improvement opportunities

All the areas for improvement in the current working relationship and practices

Agreed action	By whom	By when
Specific steps which either party will		
take to address the improvement		
opportunities		

Supplier Signature ____________ **Date agreed** ____________

Customer Signature ____________ **Review date** ____________
(to check if actions taken and performance improved)

CUSTOMER-SUPPLIER AGREEMENT: Example

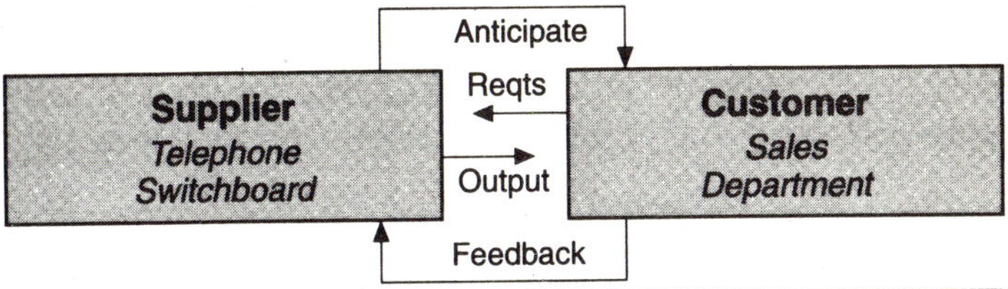

Supplier specification

To answer exchange calls within 20 seconds.
To establish nature of inquiry.
To transfer all external calls to the correct extension.

Customer requirements

To receive correct external calls from the switchboard.

Measures	**Actual**	**Target**
% calls answered after 20 seconds	*10%*	*0*
% calls transferred to incorrect extension	*20%*	*5%*

Improvement opportunities

- *Calls often transferred to the wrong extension, leads to external and internal customer frustration and delays.*
- *The directory entries are unclear, they confuse switchboard operators.*
- *The operators do not always find out the nature of the call and therefore put them through to the wrong extension.*

Agreed action	**By whom**	**By when**
1. *Sales Department to advise switchboard of correct extension numbers to use.*	*Sales Manager*	*End of week*
2. *Switchboard to obtain all relevant information from customers before transferring the call.*	*Switchboard Supervisor*	*Immediately*

Supplier *Switchboard Supervisor* **Date agreed** *22 December*
Customer *Sales Manager* **Review date** *31 January*

How it helps

A CSA can help ensure that the expectations of both customer and supplier are matched and highlight the elements which are key to maintaining or achieving the agreed output. It fosters teamwork between different departments and individuals.

> **HINT!** REMEMBER, THE PURPOSE IS TO MAKE IMPROVEMENTS IN ORDER TO STRENGTHEN CUSTOMER SUPPLIER LINKS AND NOT TO GENERATE PAPER

CSAs can become extremely complicated – often it is best to start with a simple letter of understanding and add to it as problems are exposed.

CSAs can also become overly bureaucratic. It is important that they are focused on the areas of greatest need and that paperwork is kept to a minimum.

Remove False Customers

What it is

False customers are people or departments interposing themselves between you and your real customer so acting as a postbox or filter. They add delay or cost to a specific process (this does not necessarily mean they are redundant overall!) This tool will help you to identify your false customers and gives some practical tips on how to remove or at least work around them.

How to use it

1. Identity all of your customers. Note what you supply them with, eg goods, information, advice, time. Also note what each customer does with your output, eg assembles components; makes decisions; collates figures to give overall position, etc.

Customer	Output supplied	How output is used by customer

2. Review your chart. If you do not know how your output is used, find out from your customers.

3. If you find that:

- your customers do nothing with your output
- they simply pass it to someone else
- you yourself could do what they do faster and quicker, (eg making a simple decision)

then you have uncovered a false customer!

For example: false customers

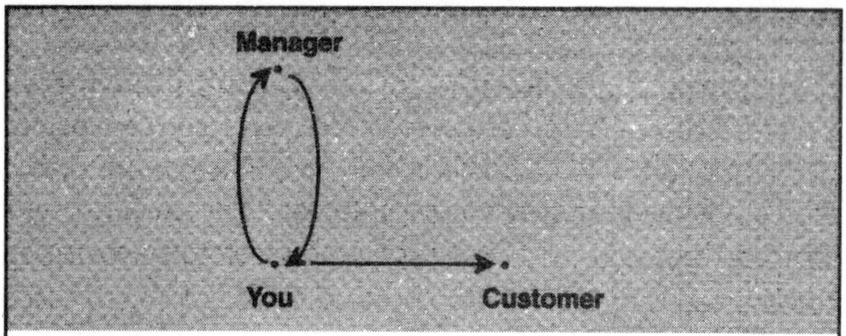

You have to check your output with your manager before speaking to your customer for no valid reason

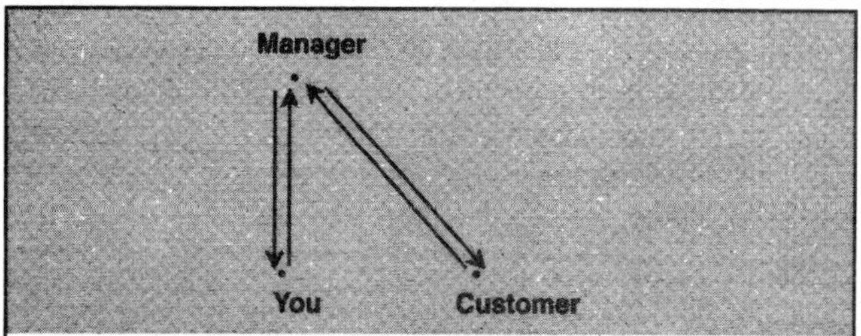

Your manager insists on channelling both the query and reply rather than you speaking directly to the customer

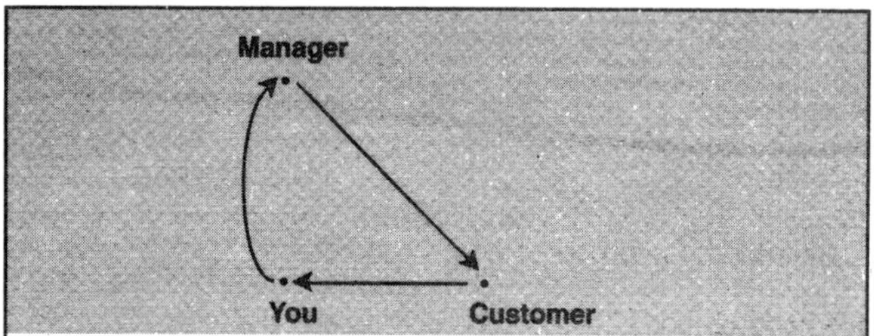

Customer contacts you directly. You have to refer all decisions to your manager who contacts the customer directly, even though you could have dealt with the problem

4. Once identified, it is important to tackle false customers sensitively and constructively. They often arise through custom and practice; local tinkering with processes or extra controls for new staff/quality problems and not just through personal empire building or a need for control.

5. You can tackle false customers by:

- asking to set up a customer-supplier agreement. This gives a structure to a discussion and will highlight unused outputs, etc
- mapping the whole process to show up dead ends or unnecessary loops
- agreeing authority levels to devolve decisions
- coaching or developing individuals to accept tasks
- ensuring all affected parties are aware of any process improvements/system enhancements, etc which turn current customers into false customers by removing the need for certain tasks/controls or decisions.

6. Finally, remember that false customers are not always someone else – it might be you! Do you always add value to the outputs you receive from your suppliers?

How it helps

Removing false customers speeds up processes, reduces costs and increases job satisfaction. This tool gives some practical ways to identify and tackle your false customers in a constructive and proactive way.

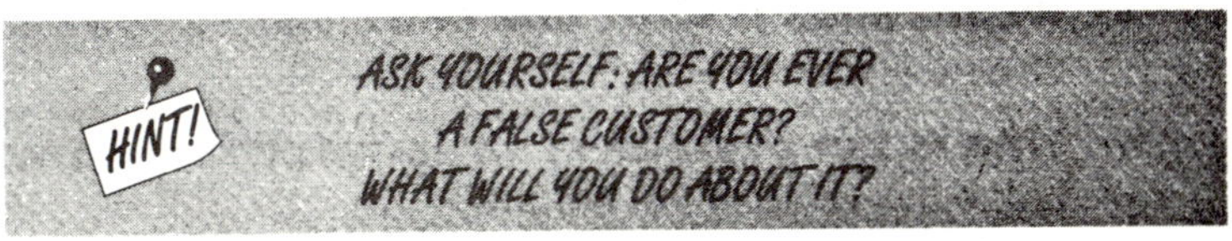

6 Manage your processes

Think Process

What it is

Process improvement starts from a mentality of accepting that everything is part of a process. Thinking in process terms is part of the revolution which starts with the leader. What are the processes I am involved in? Are they effective? How can they be made better?

This tool asks you some simple questions to help you assess how well you 'Think Process'.

How to use it

1. Work through the following questions:

- **What is my process?** – choose a small process of some significance as an example, eg order entry, message taking, authorising expenditure, organising a meeting.
- **Where does it start and end?** – put some limits around it with inputs and outputs.
- **Who is the customer?** – state the person who will judge the value of the output.
- **What are the requirements?** – specify the outputs in the customer's terms.
- **How well are they met?**– does the process do what it is supposed?... in time?... efficiently?... consistently?

- **What improvement goals?** – state what would give substantially greater value to the customer and the business.
- **What are the activities and the flow?** – list the steps the process goes through and show how they are linked.
- **Do they all add value?** – are some steps unnecessary, excessive, duplicated?
- **Can they be done more quickly?** – can some steps be combined, linked more directly, bypassed or done simultaneously?
- **Is there a radical alternative?** – forget today's process; could it be done some other way entirely?

2. What have you learned? – is there scope for multiplying value by re-engineering this process or is there gain from simply sharpening it up or slimming it down? If the scope is there for this small example, imagine the impact on a critical business process. Imagine, too, the impact on the whole business and the contribution process improvement can make to business success.
3. If you were unable to answer all of the questions what do you need to do to get the information?
4. How can you improve the way you 'think process'?

How it helps

This tool will help you to develop a strategy for improving your process(es) by highlighting the key questions you need to answer and the steps you need to take.

HINT!

REMEMBER THAT EVERYTHING YOU DO IS PART OF A PROCESS

Map Processes

What it is

A Process Map is a pictorial representation of a process, using basic flowcharting symbols. This tool will help you to identify and map your key processes.

How to use it

The basic symbols are:

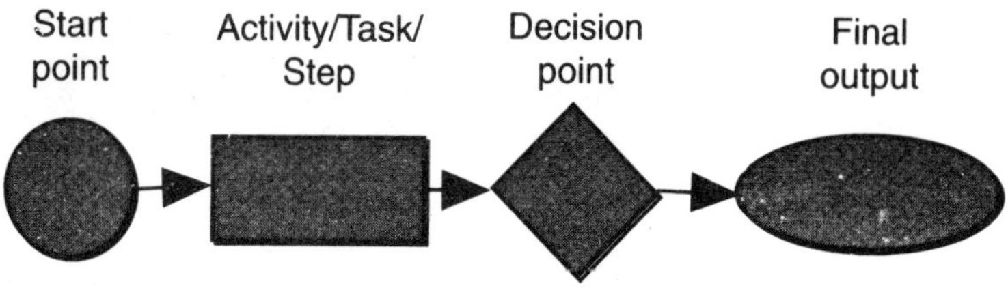

1. Identify your key processes

These should:

- be large enough to matter in terms of delivering useful output
- be small enough to map and understand
- result in output which is aimed at meeting the requirements of a customer.

> HINT! KEEP FOCUSED ON THE OVERALL PURPOSE OF THE PROCESS, OTHERWISE CHANGES MAY NOT ACHIEVE REAL IMPROVEMENT

Processes can involve many disciplines, eg developing a new product would require contributions from R&D, marketing, manufacturing; or they may be restricted to a specific area, eg updating a computer printout.

The one(s) you choose to focus on will depend on your position and level in the organisation.

HINT! SETTING CLEAR, AGREED BOUNDARIES IS VITAL – KEEP IT SIMPLE

2. Establish a process team

Assemble people who between them know the full range of activities making up the process. The team may range from a senior management group to a small number of people with similar duties. Keep the team small – you'll move much faster.

3. Set the boundaries of the process

Agree where you will start and stop for the purposes of the exercise. Choose natural break points.

4. Determine appropriate level of detail

Determine the level of detail appropriate to your improvement work. Should it be fine detail or 'the big picture'?

5. Identify all activities that make up the process

Brainstorm all the activities that make up the process. Put all ideas onto individual Post-it® Notes. This makes it easier to move them around later. Describe each activity as a noun and verb, eg 'report written'.

A simple inputs/outputs diagram can be used prior to brainstorming to help identify both the key inputs and outputs for a process and the secondary information flows in and out of the process. This helps everyone to consider the whole process when brainstorming.

HINT! BEWARE OF MUDDLING UP THE CURRENT AND IDEAL PROCESSES

6. Sequence the process activities

Use Post-it® Notes to establish the correct sequence of activities.

7. Show decision points and connections between the activities

8. Conduct a TOPIC analysis

Consider where in the process map you can add information under the following categories:

Time:

- actual time (how long does the activity take?)
- elapsed time (how long before another task must the activity be performed?)

Ownership:

- who is responsible for or influential in each part of the process?

Personnel:

- who actually carries out the task (name a specific individual or department)

Information:

- what information is needed for results from each step?

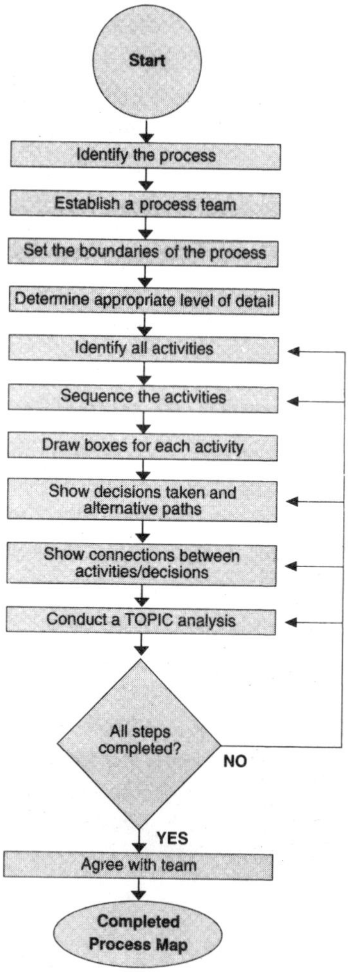

- Is any information lacking/superfluous?

Cost:

- what is the cost of each activity? How much of this cost is the result of things not being done 'right first time'.

9. Check for completeness

Ensure every activity is included, every box is connected, every decision point has at least two exits. Correct any omissions or errors.

10. Analyse the process

- Does the current process operate successfully?
- Challenge the complexity of the process.
- Can the process be simplified?
- Examine the value or benefit of each step. Are there clear Customer-Supplier Agreements?
- Where do errors and waste occur – how can they be avoided?
- Take a fresh look: 'why do we do it this way?'
- It may be necessary to collect further data using Check Sheets to complete the analysis.

11. Agree next steps

Agree who the Process Owner should be. Agree Action Plans for improving the process. See example on the next page.

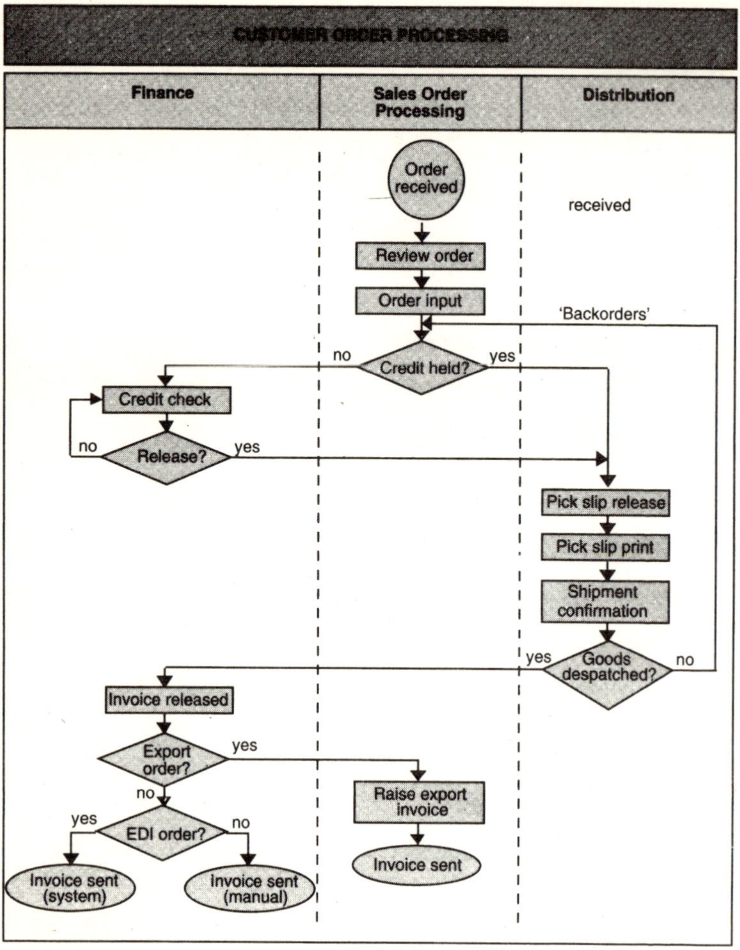

How it helps

Mapping helps you to:

- understand how a process currently operates
- manage how it currently operates
- identify and plan improvements.

Measure Processes

What it is

The purpose of measurement is to:

- ensure progress
- prevent problems and errors
- work with facts not opinions
- set standards
- recognise success.

This tool gives guidelines on effective measurement which will help to ensure you focus on the 'critical few'.

How to use it

1. Think about what you currently measure.
2. Does your current approach give you the information you need?
3. Do you have the following:
   - clear 'top-down' requirements
     - measurable improvement goals
     - specific process outputs
     - numerical targets and milestones?
   - customer-related measures
     - to clarify requirements
     - to receive ongoing feedback?
   - process performance measures which are
     - focused on key points
     - clear, simple and relevant?
   - measures of 'bottom-up' achievements
     - focused on work teams
     - compared to targets
     - visible to team members?

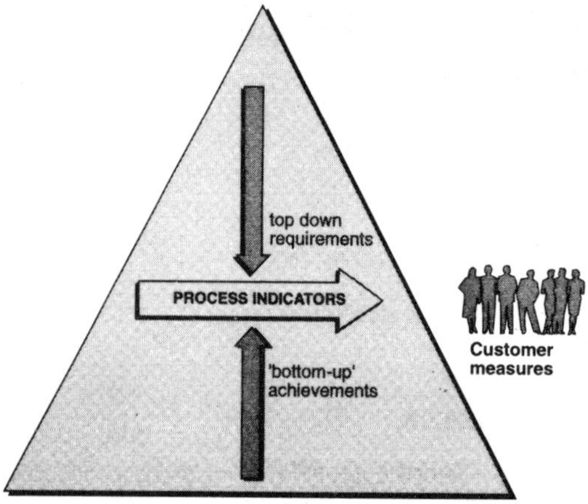

4. If not, use the following checklist to improve your approach to measurement.

Measurement guidelines

✔ **Focus on your goals**

- set SMART objectives
- link measures to what you have to achieve

✔ **Measure things as well as money**

- develop non-financial performance measures
- convert to money where it makes sense

✔ **Listen to the voice of your customer**

- what are your customer's requirements?
- what is your customer's response?
- how can you anticipate changing needs quickly?

✔ **Listen to the voice of your process**

- before; is the process capable of meeting your customer's requirements?
- during; is it delivering?
- after; did it meet your customer's requirements?

- ✔ **Measure what is wrong as well as what is right**
  - monitor non-conformance to requirements
- ✔ **Concentrate on the critical few**
  - focus on what is important for customers
  - define your priorities for developing or maintaining a competitive edge
  - identify the pulse points which will tell you if you are moving towards your mission
- ✔ **Self track and report**
  - have teams/individuals create their own measures
  - have teams/individuals track their own performance
- ✔ **Display the data**
  - make the data visible
  - ensure data is timely
- ✔ **Be consistent**
  - avoid frequent changes

How it helps

Measurement is crucial to knowing (as opposed to guessing or assuming) where you are and how you compare to your targets and goals. There is a danger, however, of becoming swamped in data which clogs rather than clarifies. This tool gives a set of guidelines for effective measurement as a basis for improving results.

HINT! *MEASURES CAN INFLUENCE THE WAY PEOPLE BEHAVE. CHOOSE THEM CAREFULLY!*

Display Performance Data

What it is

One of the key principles of effective measurement is to display performance data so that everyone knows how they are doing and the contribution they are making (or otherwise) to achieving the overall goals.

The *Solve that problem!* Toolbox gives details of how to construct types of charts (see Data Display). This tool focuses more on the use of charts to energise and recognise improvement.

How to use it

1. Identify the key performance measures for your team/department/location/company.
2. Ensure that you are able to collect or provide regular, accurate and timely information on these measures at an acceptable cost.
3. Design an appropriate pro forma for displaying the measures. Make it as big and colourful and clear as possible. (An example is shown on the next page).
4. Take steps to ensure that everyone in the area understands the measures; why they are important and what they contribute to them. (If necessary, break this into a series of briefings over time so it is in digestible form.)
5. Agree who is going to be responsible for updating the chart (share this among several people if appropriate).
6. Ensure that the charts are always up to date and accurate.
7. Run through the latest figures at regular team meetings/briefings to highlight the successes and agree how to tackle problems.

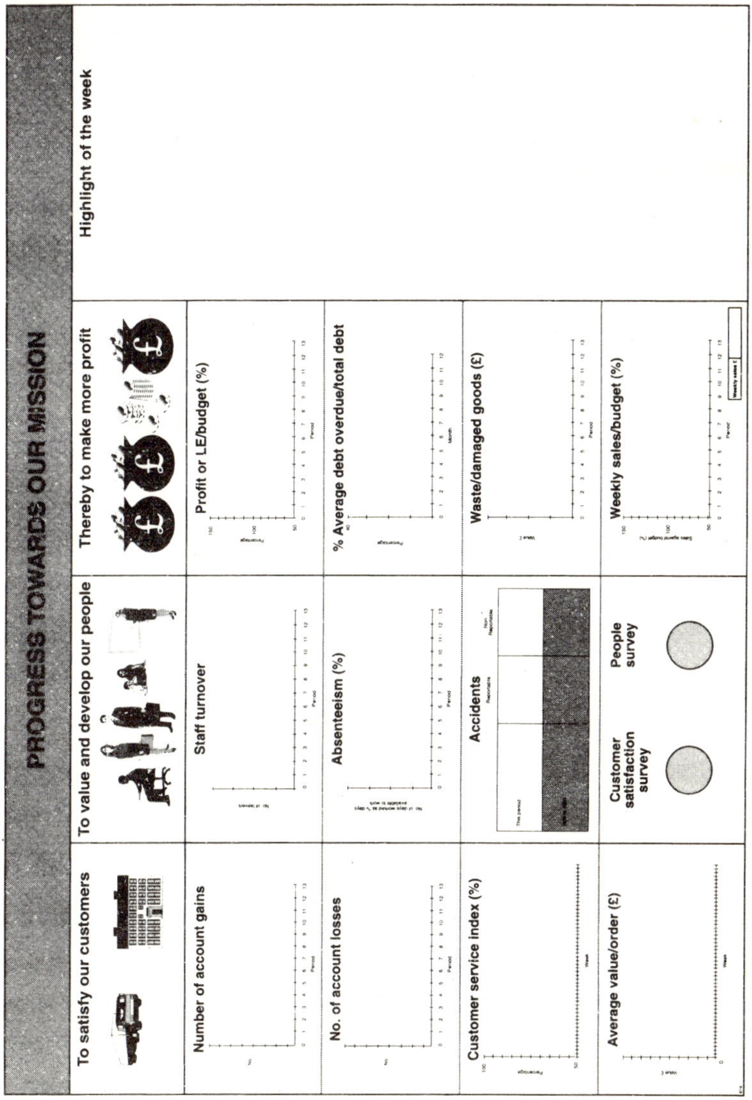
PROGRESS TOWARDS OUR MISSION
To satisfy our customers
To value and develop our people
Thereby to make more profit
Highlight of the week
Number of account gains
Staff turnover
Profit or LE/budget (%)
No. of account losses
Absenteeism (%)
% Average debt overdue/total debt
Customer service index (%)
Accidents
Waste/damaged goods (£)
Average value/order (£)
Customer satisfaction survey
People survey
Weekly sales/budget (%)

8. Use shortfalls in the measures as a starting point for improvement projects and/or suggestions for improvements.

HINT! BEWARE OF BEING TOO 'GLOSSY' – PEOPLE LIKE OWNERSHIP OF CHARTS; SO ALLOW HAND WRITTEN NOTES, ETC – IT MAKES IT PERSONAL

How it helps

Colourful and clear display charts bring performance to life. They give feedback on progress; provide recognition of success and highlight the areas to tackle to improve performance. They are therefore a useful tool for change.

Analyse Processes

What it is

Once you understand today's processes (by mapping) and know how well they perform (by measurement), you and your team are ready to analyse the processes as the next step towards improving their performance. This tool contains a simple checklist for analysing processes and shows where this fits into the overall process improvement framework.

How to use it

1. Decide which process to work on, eg most important to customers/most wasteful/biggest user of resources.
2. Map the current process and collect performance data.
3. Use the following checklist to analyse the process:

Analysing the process

- ✔ Where are the delays?
- ✔ Where is there duplication?
- ✔ Where is the bottleneck?
- ✔ What are the unnecessary steps?
- ✔ Where are the unnecessary checks?
- ✔ How productive is it?
- ✔ How efficient is it?
- ✔ How wasteful is it?
- ✔ Is the layout efficient (desk, cell, floor, etc)?
- ✔ Is there effort wasted on unnecessary movement?
- ✔ What are the recurrent errors and mistakes?
- ✔ How do the operators feel about it?

✔ How does it compare to others?

✔ Is it measured or are you guessing?

And most important of all ...

✔ Does it consistently meet your customer's needs?

4. Use the output from your analysis to generate ideas for improvement.

5. Use an appropriate tool to decide which improvement(s) to implement.

6. Map the improved process.

This tool gives a simple overview to process improvement. The *Solve that problem!* Toolbox contains a more detailed methodology. The 13 steps of the PLAN-DO-CHECK-ACT cycle guide you through the problem solving process while the matrix shows which tools are most appropriate at each step. This is summarised on the following page:

Steps of process improvement		Which tools to use: Action Plan	Asking Why Five Times	Benchmarking	Brainstorming	Cause & Effect Analysis	Check Sheets	Consensus Reaching	Control Charts	Cost Benefit Analysis	Customer-Supplier Agreements	Data Display	Decision Charts	Force Field Analysis	Gantt Chart	Pareto Analysis	Performance Expectation Grid	Process Mapping	Time/Cost Analysis
PLAN	1. Define the process				✔														
	2. Specify the customer's requirements										✔						✔		
	3. Collect performance data						✔		✔			✔					✔	✔	
	4. Analyse the process		✔			✔										✔	✔		✔
	5a. Identify benchmarks	✔		✔	✔														
	5b. Identify step-by-step improvements				✔			✔		✔									
	5c. Identify breakthroughs			✔	✔			✔										✔	
	6. Evaluate alternatives							✔		✔									
	7a. Redesign the process																	✔	
	7b. Develop an implementation plan	✔			✔									✔	✔				
DO	8. Implement plan	✔													✔				
CHECK	9. Monitor performance evaluation against plan	✔																	
	10. Identify reasons for deviations	✔					✔						✔						
ACT	11. Take corrective action for deviations	✔																	
	12. Standardise in the process – make a successful solution permanent	✔			✔						✔								
	13. Review	✔			✔					✔							✔		

How it helps

Rigorous analysis and the use of disciplined improvement techniques facilitate effective process improvement. This tool gives an overview of the method and tools available in the *Solve that problem!* Toolbox and an additional checklist for process analysis:

Reduce Waste

What it is

Waste is a result of unclear customer requirements, inefficient processes or error. It is therefore costly and frustrating and can lead to customer dissatisfaction.

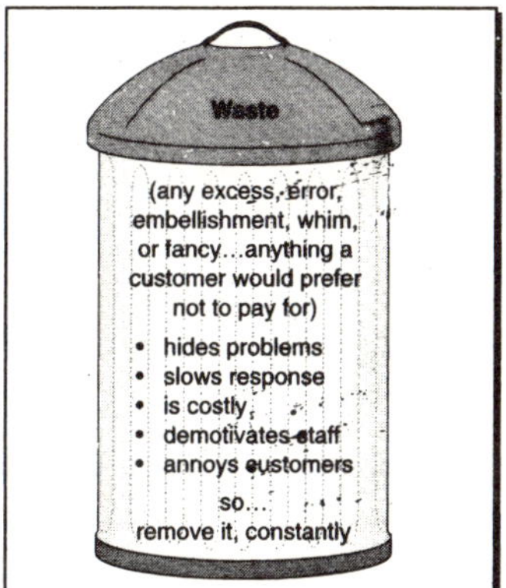

Waste is everywhere in an organisation

This tool outlines a method for identifying the costs of waste in the form of external and internal failure costs. It then outlines the two strategies for removing or reducing waste, namely inspection and prevention and the type of activities they both involve.

How to use it

1. Review the following checklist and identify the types of waste you have in your department or organisation.

Examples of external failure costs – once problems have reached the external customer:

✔ Training costs for repair personnel

✔ Downtime charges

✔ Product recall

✔ Notification delays and costs

- ✔ Complaint-handling costs
- ✔ Cost of products rejected and returned
- ✔ Warranty expenses and claims
- ✔ Cost to re-inspect and re-test
- ✔ Cost of corrective actions
- ✔ Direct customer contact on field problems
- ✔ Handling returned material
- ✔ Returned-materials reports
- ✔ Failure reports
- ✔ Cashflow costs of legitimate late payments
- ✔ Credit notes
- ✔ Loss of sales if existing customers go elsewhere

Examples of internal failure costs – before problems reach the external customer:

- ✔ Installation failure costs
- ✔ Downgrading (substandard product) cost/concessions
- ✔ Overtime because of problems
- ✔ Scrap or rework (including labour costs)
- ✔ Re-inspection because of rejects
- ✔ Failure reports and analysis
- ✔ Abandoned programmes
- ✔ Billing-error costs
- ✔ Payroll-error costs
- ✔ Incorrect accounting entry costs
- ✔ Purchase order rewrite costs

- ✔ All expediting costs
- ✔ Improper payments to suppliers
- ✔ Rework of supplier parts
- ✔ Excess inventory because of non-dependable supplier deliveries/quality
- ✔ Accidents, injuries
- ✔ Costs because of waiting (eg meeting not starting on time)
- ✔ Efforts to fix blame
- ✔ Time lost because reports are wrong
- ✔ Cost of unused reports
- ✔ Cost of trying to meet bad estimates
- ✔ Order lost because bids were received too late
- ✔ Lost sales because telephones are not answered promptly
- ✔ Cost of not following procedures
- ✔ Sales lost because of stock shortages
- ✔ Cost of stopping production because of poor quality output
- ✔ Redirecting incorrectly addressed mail
- ✔ All correction activity
- ✔ Equipment failure
- ✔ Re-inspection, re-testing

2. Calculate roughly the total cost of this waste per year to your organisation.

3. Review the checklists on prevention and appraisal to identify what you currently do in these areas and their annual cost.

Examples of prevention costs – getting it 'right first time'

- ✔ Education and training
- ✔ Defect-prevention activities
- ✔ Process design
- ✔ Developing Quality systems, procedures and standards
- ✔ Software planning
- ✔ Automation planning to reduce defects
- ✔ Activities that will prevent an error from recurring
- ✔ Preventive maintenance
- ✔ Operator/inspector qualifications
- ✔ Assistance to suppliers on quality training
- ✔ Quality awareness activities
- ✔ Zero-defect programmes
- ✔ Elements of product design
- ✔ Process improvement activities
- ✔ Planning
- ✔ Establishing customer requirements
- ✔ Production trials
- ✔ Calibration and maintenance of production equipment used to evaluate quality
- ✔ Supplier assurance (assessment, audit and surveillance)
- ✔ Design and development of quality measurement

Examples of appraisal costs – checking to see if work has been done 'right first time':

- ✔ Product quality audits
- ✔ Quality systems audits
- ✔ Verifying workmanship standards
- ✔ Checking
- ✔ Data processing inspection and test reports
- ✔ Process surveillance at suppliers
- ✔ Incoming inspection activities
- ✔ Employee inspection of completed work
- ✔ Surveying customer satisfaction
- ✔ Measuring effectiveness
- ✔ Pre-production, acceptance/testing/verification
- ✔ Field tests
- ✔ Stock evaluation
- ✔ Laboratory acceptance testing
- ✔ Inspection and test equipment
- ✔ Materials consumed during inspection and testing
- ✔ Analysis and reporting of inspection results
- ✔ Approvals and endorsements by outside bodies
- ✔ Record storage

4. You can now calculate in broad terms your overall Cost of Quality.

Failure/waste costs £ ____________	}	Annual Cost of Quality £ ____________
Prevention/appraisal costs £ ____________		

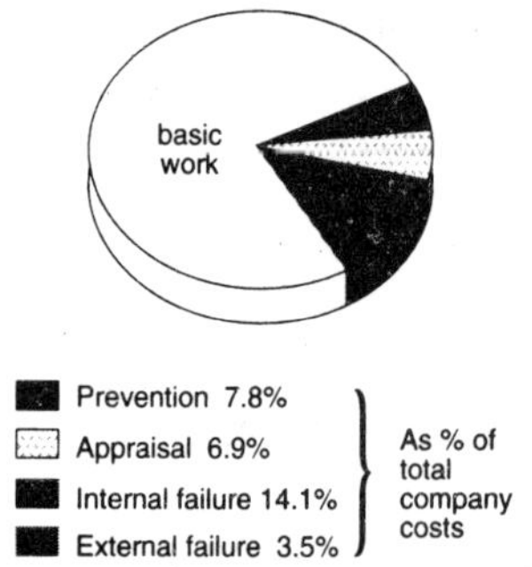

A typical Cost of Quality summary

5. Again, review the checklists on prevention and appraisal. Identify the areas that you could work on to reduce your waste.

6. Review your main sources of waste. Does this highlight particular processes which would benefit from focused improvement activity?

7. Agree with your team your priorities, strategy and first steps in tackling waste in your area.

8. Check that any increases in spending on prevention and appraisal costs are more than paid for by reductions in waste costs. You should see this effect:

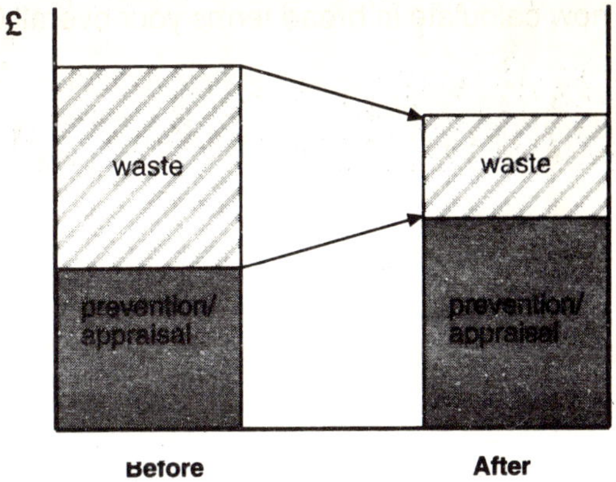

How it helps

Waste is expensive and frustrating and stops you doing other more valuable things. This tool will help you to identify your areas of waste and to develop an action plan to tackle them based on increased prevention and inspection. Using this tool will reduce your overall cost of quality, save time and improve satisfaction (for both customers and employees).

7 Help others to change

Make the Most of People

What it is

This tool will help you to assess your approach to others and the areas you need to work on. Unless you really believe that others have an important contribution to make to effective change, your behaviours and attitude will undermine your plans.

How to use it

1. Review the following questions:

- **Do you respect people as individuals?**– everyone has the potential to contribute more and will respond to being treated as a thinking person.
- **Do you use teams? ... lots of them?** – teams stimulate and encourage people beyond their individual talents; but teams only work well with good team disciplines.
- **Are you capturing people's ideas?** – expect people to give you improvement ideas ... and then use them.
- **Do you display performance and progress?** – visibility encourages an environment of challenge and healthy competition and also makes it easier to spread ideas and to recognise contribution.
- **Do you encourage sharing?** – help people to help each other improve.
- **Are you developing partners?** – partnerships extend the teamwork well beyond organisational boundaries.

- **Do you give time for prevention?** – time to think and plan generates much more time later.
- **Are you recognising?** – catch people doing good things and show them that you are interested and value what they are doing.
- **Are you making people more valuable?** – encourage people to take responsibility, to challenge to add skills, to learn new methods ... to develop their own ideas.
- **Are you doing it too?** – improvement is not a way of life in your company unless you are doing it as well.

2. Could you answer 'yes' to all 10 questions?

If not, which ones do you feel you need to work on the most?

3. Identify which specific tools you can use to help you make the most of other people.

How it helps

It is often said that people are an organisation's greatest asset. This tool will help you assess how well you are growing and nurturing this asset.

Use Teamwork

What it is

When people work closely together they can:

- share knowledge and experience
- break down functional and hierarchical divides
- reduce the sense of isolation or insecurity in the face of change, 'we're in it together'
- challenge each others' assumptions and prejudices
- apply group problem–solving tools
- make faster progress than when working alone
- have more fun!

These benefits of teamworking are unfortunately not available for free – they must be worked on and developed.

This tool simply gives a taste of the range of tools included in the *Build that team!* Toolbox. You should refer to the full Toolbox to find out how to go about the steps listed.

How to use it

1. Review the following process on the next page which is typical for project teams.

2. Which stage are you at?

3. What issues or problems are you grappling with?

- Getting started?
- Building the team?
- Working together?
- Reviewing performance?
- Disbanding the team?
- Improving work teams?

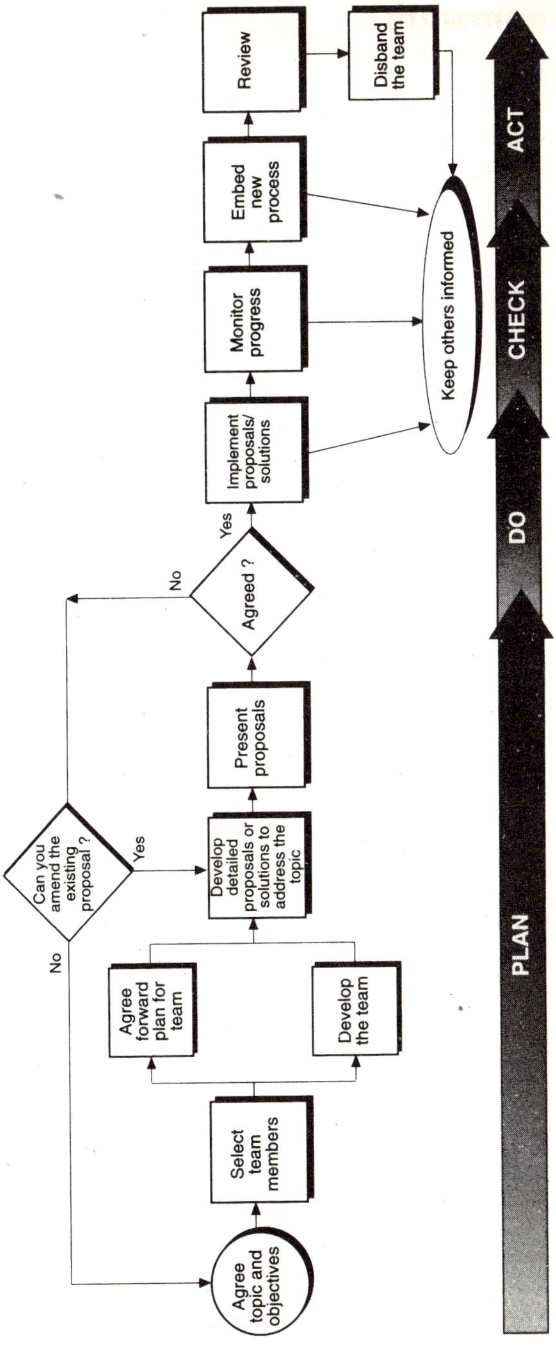

Agree topic and objectives
Select team members
Agree forward plan for team
Develop the team
Develop detailed proposals or solutions to address the topic
Present proposals
Agreed ?
Yes
No
Can you amend the existing proposal ?
Yes
No
Implement proposals/ solutions
Monitor progress
Embed new process
Review
Disband the team
Keep others informed
PLAN
DO
CHECK
ACT

4. Use the *Build that team!* Toolbox to identify specific tools available to help you.

How it helps

Teamworking is increasingly used as a tool for bringing about change rapidly and also for overcoming some of the downsides of change such as insecurity and resistance. Teams can be permanent or temporary; single or multi-functional; small or large. This tool outlines the range of tools available in the *Build that team!* Toolbox and their place in creating the difference.

Coach

What it is

Coaching is a process by which a team leader or fellow team member through direct discussion, questioning and guided activities, helps a person to do a task better than would otherwise have been the case. It helps to achieve both performance improvement and individual development. It deals with the knowledge, skills, competence and confidence needed to perform specific tasks/work in real work situations.

How to use it

The coaching process consists of a number of key stages:
To coach effectively you need to follow each of the stages in this checklist:

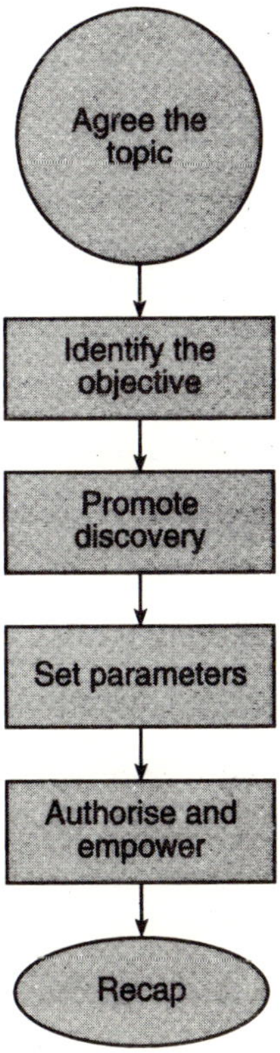

1. Agree the topic

- What is the topic/project you would like to delegate and coach another individual to do? Agree this with the person concerned (coachee!).

2. Identify the objectives

- What is your long term objective? eg "That in six weeks I'll have put forward costed recommendations for moving the office to Manchester."

  Discuss and agree this, ensuring it is a SMART objective.
- What would you like to learn/gain from each coaching session?
- How long do you think you will both need to achieve this?

3. Promote discovery – the current position

Encourage your coachee to research and investigate the current position.

- What is the present situation?
- What has been done already?
- What happened as a result of that?
- What evidence is there that this problem exists?
- Who else has this experience?
- Where exactly does the problem lie?
- When does this problem occur?
- Who else is involved/responsible?
- How do they see the situation?

4. Promote discovery – the options

Ask your coachee to come up with a number of options and encourage him to evaluate the consequences of adopting each one. Ask him:

- what options have you thought of?

- what would be the first step?
- what would be the consequences for, eg staffing, budget, other departments?
- how have others tackled this in the past?
- what are the pay-offs/costs of these options?
- which option do you think is most viable?

5. Set parameters

Establish exactly what needs to be done and by when. Ensure the coachee knows how far he can go without reference to you – don't assume he understands.

6. Authorise and empower

Ensure others know you have authorised your coachee to do the agreed work/research, otherwise they may quickly hit barriers to cooperation.

Ensure they have the resources, eg transport, expenses and administrative support, to carry out their task.

7. **Recap**

At the end of each session, agree the following to ensure you both understand:

- what are the next steps?
- what steps are *you* going to take?
- when will he do that?
- what are the obstacles?
- what could stop him achieving this?
- what support does he need?
- who can he enlist to support him?

How it helps

Coaching helps achieve both performance improvement and employee development. It is an important tool in achieving empowerment, improving morale and releasing management time.

Empower

What it is

Empowerment is one of the buzz–words of the 90's and is often overused to suggest a general letting–go of authority. It is, in fact, a disciplined devolution of decision–making underpinned by both a clear framework of practical support and a value system that believes that everyone has more to offer and greater potential to fulfil if given the opportunity and appropriate environment. Empowerment is therefore about helping everyone to give of their best.

This tool uses a questionnaire to outline the practical framework that needs to be in place for empowerment to succeed. The key areas covered are:

- Goals and measures
- Job and organisation design
- Knowledge and skills
- Management support
- Recognition.

How to use it

1. Complete the following questionnaire focusing on the individual or team(s) you wish to empower. (For 'you' read they or he/she).
2. Give the individual or team a copy (or work through it with them) so they can give their perceptions.
3. Identify and/or agree the areas you need to work on.
4. Agree on an action plan to move forward.

For each of the questions listed below, choose a response from the range:

- [4] Very satisfied
- [3] Satisfied
- [2] Slightly dissatisfied
- [1] Dissatisfied
- [0] Not applicable

Enter your response in the box against each question. Please do not enter anything other than one of these responses. Do not dwell on the questions; it should take no more than 15 minutes to complete them all. Only answer 'very satisfied' if all parts of the question are true.

How satisfied are you that........

1. You have very stretching, clear targets to achieve ☐
2. You feel part of a team/have a sense of belonging/loyalty ☐
3. You are able to get appropriate education and training to develop yourself and are encouraged and supported to do so ☐
4. You are thanked personally for a job well done (by your customers/suppliers/managers/peers) ☐
5. Your manager regularly reviews your training needs with you and takes action as a result ☐
6. You are involved in setting your targets ☐
7. You have sufficient contact with your customers and receive useful feedback and data on requirements ☐
8. You are encouraged to come up with improvements and to take appropriate action as a result ☐

9. You have measures that tell you how well you are doing and you use them to identify improvements ☐

10. Team as well as individual achievements are recognised ☐

11. You can speak up about your mistakes and this is received constructively ☐

12. You are encouraged to challenge the status quo and your manager listens generously to your views and ideas ☐

13. You are able to make day-to-day decisions about your work to meet your customers' needs and are encouraged to do so ☐

14. You understand how achieving your targets will contribute to the overall goals of the company ☐

15. You receive feedback from your customers (internal and external) on your performance without asking ☐

16. You are asked to provide input to future team plans and strategies ☐

17. You feel appropriately recognised for your achievements ☐

18. You have all the right knowledge and skills to do your job ☐

19. You feel able to speak to your manager about problems and concerns and you are really listened to ☐

20. Your manager praises you when you do well and gives you constructive feedback on areas for improvement ☐

21. You have all the resources you need to do your job (eg equipment, materials) ☐

22. You receive active help and encouragement from your manager to improve your knowledge and skills ☐

23. Your manager understands your values and ambitions and takes steps to help you fulfil them ☐

24. You are clear about the limits of your decision-making authority ☐

25. When necessary, you can take decisions which exceed your normal authority without reference to your manager (provided you can justify your actions). ☐

Now score your answers: transfer each response to the appropriate box listed under the five dimensions:

	Job design	Knowledge & skills	Goals & measures	Management support	Recognition & reward
	2 ☐	3 ☐	1 ☐	12 ☐	4 ☐
	7 ☐	5 ☐	6 ☐	19 ☐	10 ☐
	13 ☐	8 ☐	9 ☐	22 ☐	15 ☐
	21 ☐	11 ☐	14 ☐	23 ☐	17 ☐
	24 ☐	18 ☐	16 ☐	25 ☐	20 ☐
Totals:	____	____	____	____	____

The total scores for each dimension can then be shown on a chart and comparisons made between the views of different team members, if appropriate:

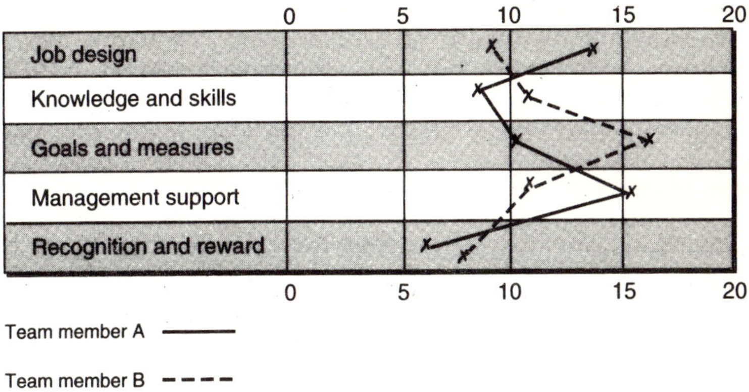

How it helps

Empowerment is for many people a rather vague concept. This questionnaire will help you to assess more clearly both the overall level of empowerment and specific areas where it may be appropriate to develop it further.

Use Team Briefing

What it is

Team Briefing is a system of regular meetings to pass on management information to all employees. To enable this to happen quickly and effectively, a schedule is established with dates, times and places for named groups to meet with their 'team briefers'; these briefers are the team leaders for that group of people.

Team Briefing is a normal part of the manager's or supervisor's job as a communicator. It does not replace other forms of existing management communications – it complements them. The objective is to make sure that people know what is happening and why through explanation, questions and answers. It is not a group grievance session or an opportunity to discipline everyone!

Once established, Team Briefing normally takes place routinely every month, like monthly accounts. It involves everybody in attending a monthly meeting. Those who brief will also lead a meeting once a month.

This tool outlines a typical briefing process.

How to use it

1. Throughout the month, all briefers should collect snippets of information and facts on team progress in briefing folders. Two or three days before the briefing date, every briefer should write out a local team brief. The information will be about Progress, People, Policy and Points for Action.
2. The senior managers or the executives of the company should meet first for their team briefing which is normally no longer than 30 minutes.

3. Three or four items relevant to everyone should be typed on to a briefing note and copies made for all briefers. This is often referred to as the Core Brief.

4. Managers or executives from that meeting should meet and brief their teams. They should brief and explain the items on the core brief, answering any questions. Any questions that cannot be answered at the meeting should be answered as quickly as possible (normally within 48 hours). The team will take their own notes of each item as relevant and answers to questions.

5. These briefers then add this core information to their own briefs, making sure that it is all relevant. They will then brief their own teams in the same way as they were briefed.

Typical subjects for team briefing:

There is no such thing as a perfect agenda. One very useful way of thinking about the content of your brief is to divide it up into the 4 P's as suggested by The Industrial Society.

Progress

Output figures
Success stories
Customer complaints
Quality figures
Raw material usage
New orders/customers

People

Promotions
Appointments
Retirements
Visitors
Conference plans
Long service awards

Policy

Investment plans
Overtime levels
Policy changes
Improvements to facilities, eg canteen

Points for action

Training plans
Housekeeping
Health and safety
New working methods, etc

6. At the final level of briefing, notes will not normally be distributed as these are only aids to the briefer. There is no reason, however, why everyone shouldnot have access to the briefer's 'briefing file' if they wish.

7. As far as possible, the majority of the staff should be briefed at the same time or within as short a space as possible. Otherwise the grapevine takes over and diminishes the effect of team briefing.

Team briefing should be:

- ✔ In small teams
- ✔ Regular
- ✔ Done by the team leader
- ✔ Relevant
- ✔ Monitored
- ✔ Comprehensive
- ✔ Concise
- ✔ Quick
- ✔ Two-way

8. After the meetings, briefers need to obtain answers to unanswered questions and feedback the reply. They also need to keep a note of absentees and brief them as soon as they return.

9. After the system has been established it will need to be monitored to ensure timely delivery, 100% coverage, relevant material, quality of briefing, etc.

How it helps

Team briefing is a structured communication process to ensure everyone receives accurate, timely and relevant information which affects them in their job. It is a two–way mechanism and is an opportunity for seeking feedback, for raising questions and concerns and for debating implications.

Match Your Messages and Media

What it is

Communication is a difficult and complex issue in organisations simply because of the range of topics to be covered; the host of methods available and the filtering of any form of communication through individual's values, expectations and perceptions.

This tool outlines an approach to matching messages and media developed by Bill Quirke in his book Communicating Change.

How to use it

Different communication processes achieve different objectives:

Matching methods to objectives

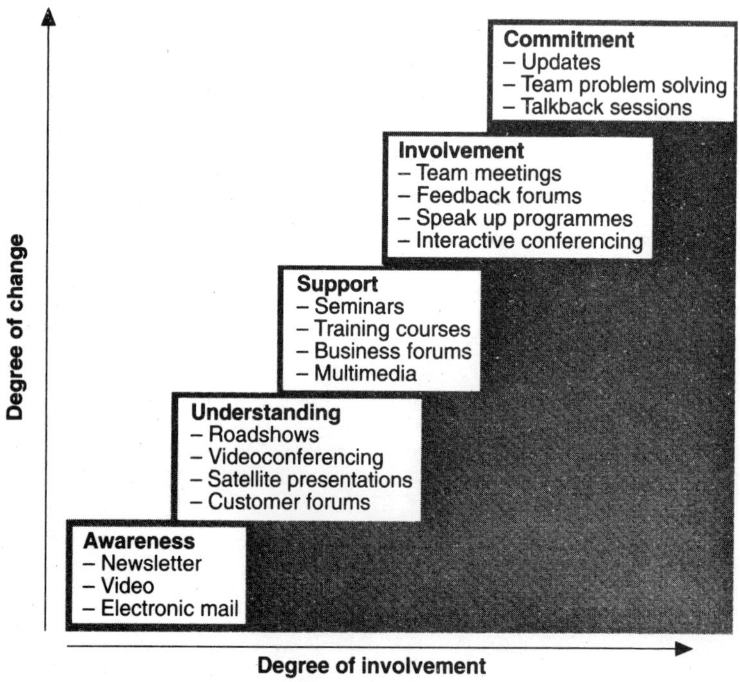

Responsibility for these different types of communication is usually:

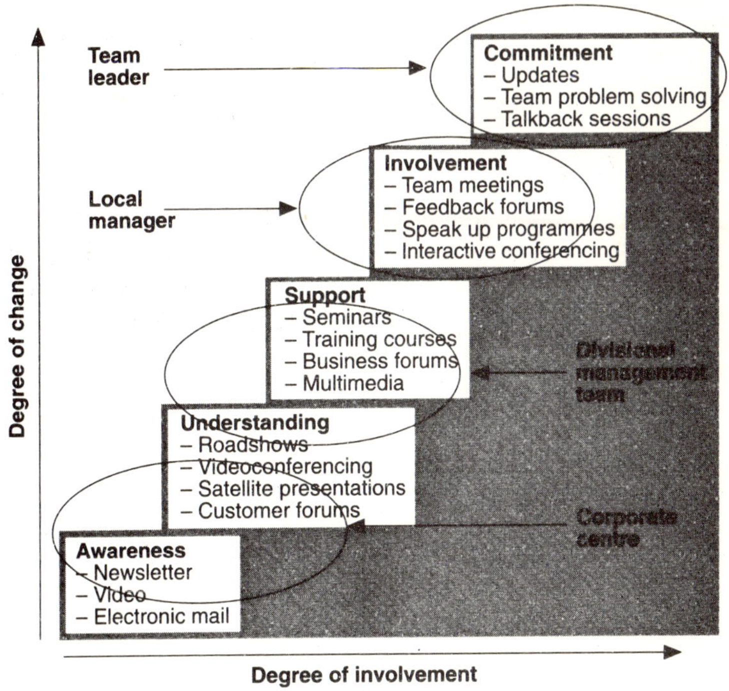

In order to plan the best communication for the specific change you wish to make:

1. Identify what degree of involvement is appropriate

- Awareness?
- Understanding?
- Support?
- Involvement?
- Commitment?

2. Identify the range of media available to you at this level.

3. Decide which media to use in this specific instance given the timeframe, cost, resources needed, etc.
4. Agree who is to be responsible for developing the media or content.
5. Develop an action plan to make it happen.

How it helps

Effective communication is vital in a changing environment if resources are to be channelled appropriately and individuals enthused to contribute. This tool outlines what can be achieved by different types of communication and the range of media available at each level.

8 Be disciplined

Assess How Well You Are Doing at Disciplined Improvement

What it is

Without discipline, improvement will be chaotic, disorganised and less effective than it could be.

This tool will help you to assess quickly how disciplined your current approach is and to highlight which of the more specific tools are most relevant to you.

How to use it

1. Review the following questions:
   - **Are processes managed as well as functions?** – process management can have more impact on a business than functional excellence.
   - **Are projects directed and reviewed against laid-down criteria?** – projects should achieve results ... results which should benefit the customer.
   - **Is teamwork developed and exploited?** – people will try harder and achieve more in teams; many business needs are better addressed by teams.
   - **Are benchmarks used?** – benchmarks reveal the gaps and the potential; use them to stir up dissatisfaction with current performance.
   - **Do departments agree explicit service contracts with each other?** – without specific agreements, people will make assumptions, losing clarity and energy.

- **Are procedures written down and published?** – when someone has found a better way, make sure it is documented and used; don't leave it in that person's head.
- **Is the management process defined and are managers assessed against it?** – don't tolerate management muddle; require your managers to be skilled and practised at setting objectives, developing plans and reviewing performance.
- **Is 'followership' practised?** – only one leader per team is needed; others should follow agreed methods and plans.
- **Do people know what being professional means?** – define the standards you expect from people representing the business.
- **Is all improvement activity integrated together?** – orchestrate the improvement disciplines for maximum impact.

2. To which questions have you had to answer "No"?

3. Which of these are the most significant weaknesses?

4. Even if you answered "yes", which areas need strengthening?

5. How can you use this Toolbox to help you take action?

How it helps

This Tool gives an overview of the disciplines available to implement effective change. Use it to identify the areas you need to work on to improve.

Apply Team Purpose Analysis

What it is

Team Purpose Analysis is a process which helps a team or unit:

- define its purpose and align with the business strategy and goals
- define the requirements, measurements and working relationships with its customers and suppliers
- identify its key processes and performance measures
- carry out an activity/task analysis to show what is currently being done and why
- identify whether or not each activity meets specific customer requirements and is right first time
- make immediate gains
- identify improvement projects for action.

In doing so, it introduces structure and priority to the improvement process so focusing and maintaining energy.

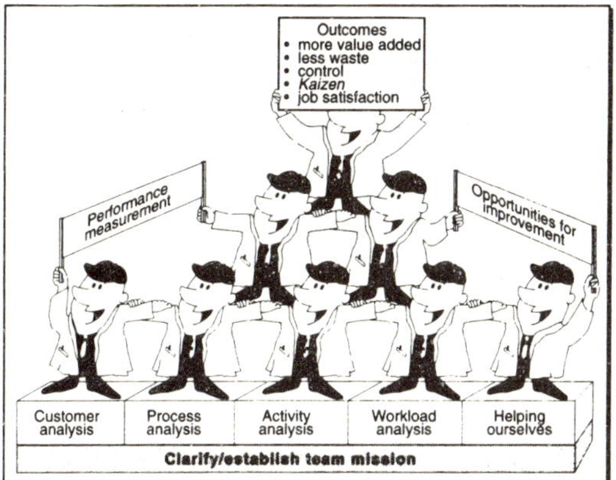

Team Purpose Analysis

Team purpose analysis (also known as departmental purpose analysis) brings together some improvement techniques to focus on what a team is doing and how it can do better. The important element is that the team does all the analysis (with the help of a facilitator at first). It can be very motivating and provides good outcomes.

How to use it

Over several months a team works through all or some of eight steps (depending on needs and priorities) addressing the following questions at each step:

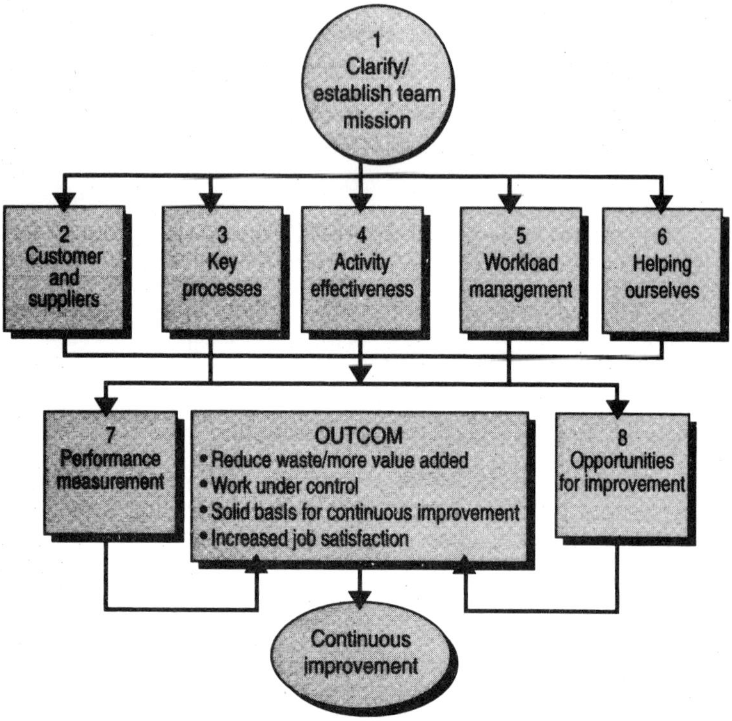

1. Clarify/establish team mission

- What is the overall mission and what are the goals of the organisation?
- What is our contribution or role in achieving this mission?
- What are our overall responsibilities and main outputs?
- So what is our team mission?

2. **Review customers and suppliers**
   - Who are our customers/suppliers?
   - What are their/our requirements?
   - What is our/their current performance?
   - What measures/feedback mechanisms exist?
   - How can outputs/inputs/measures be improved?
3. **Review processes**
   - What are our key processes?
   - Are they mapped?
   - Are our performance measures adequate?
   - How can our processes be improved?
4. **Detailed activity analysis (on key processes to be improved)**
   - How long do they take?
   - How much do they cost?
   - Where is the waste?
   - How often do things happen/go wrong?
   - How well do we use our resources?
   - Do effort and results seem in balance?
   - What should we start/stop/do differently?
5. **Workload management analysis**
   - What are our workload volumes?
   - What are the daily/weekly/monthly/annual variations and trends?
   - How well do we predict and/or manage variation?
   - How well do we balance workload and resource?
   - How can we improve our workload management?

6. Helping ourselves (internal processes)

- Are our individual roles/responsibilities sufficiently clear and coordinated?
- How well do we document our procedures and record our work?
- Do we meet our training needs sufficiently well?
- How well do we communicate with each other?
- How could we improve our teamworking?

7. Performance measures

Taking into account topics 1-6:

- What are our overall performance measures?
- Is sufficient, timely information available on these to take prompt action?

8. Opportunities for improvement

- What is the range of opportunities?
- What is urgent?
- How do we fix it?
- Can we make step by step improvements?
- What is in most need of a radical breakthrough improvement?
- Do we need to benchmark ourselves?
- How shall we prioritise the bigger issues?
- Who is going to do what?
- How will we review our progress?

HINT! YOU DON'T HAVE TO COMPLETE STEPS 1-7 BEFORE DOING SOME OF 8!

How it helps

Team Purpose Analysis helps a team focus, prioritise and organise improvement activity. It helps to ensure that customer requirements are met, processes are managed, waste is removed and the team works effectively together. Unlike many of the other tools, which take minutes or hours, TPA is an ongoing process over many months.

Benchmarking

What it is

Benchmarking is the process of learning from others as a basis for setting stretch goals, identifying breakthrough processes and accelerating improvement towards world class performance standards.

How to use it

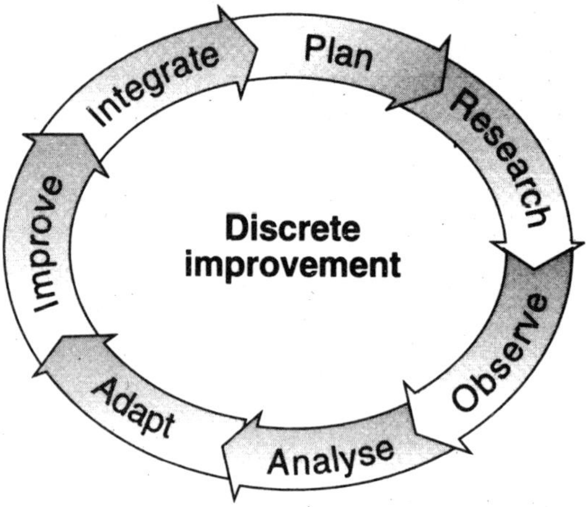

Benchmarking follows a simple, 7–step process:

1. **Plan** – Decide what to benchmark, when to do it, who to involve and what other resource will be required.
2. **Research** – Internally identify existing performance standards and processes.

   Externally identify who to benchmark against and collect as much data as possible from, eg trade press, libraries, contacts, and product literature. Don't forget you may be able to benchmark against other companies/divisions in your group.

3. **Observe** – Where possible, visit to observe and test the data collected.
4. **Analyse** – Dig into the data and observations to identify learning points and new approaches. Compare with your own existing performance. Set yourself stretch goals using what you have learnt.
5. **Adapt** – Adapt the process, techniques, tools etc that you have observed to fit your circumstances and meet your goals.
6. **Improve** – Identify ways in which the new process/product can be further improved or enhanced so that you exceed, rather than equal the benchmark.
7. **Integrate** – Implement the new process/product rigorously and ensure alignment with other processes and activities. Amend schedules/jobs/layouts etc to ensure the new way is fully integrated into the business.

Examples of benchmarking:

- An insurance company benchmarked an electricity utility in order to improve their direct debit process.
- A pager manufacturer benchmarked a pizza parlour to improve rapid, local deliveries.
- A manufacturer benchmarked Formula 1 pit teams to improve tool change-over times.

How it helps

Benchmarking is used to systematically:

- identify stretch goals for being world class
- identify ways of achieving improved performance
- help an organisation to learn from others.

Apply Plan-Do-Check-Act and Appropriate Tools

What it is

Improvement is more than just problem solving; to succeed it must become a disciplined ongoing activity. The Improvement Cycle (PLAN-DO-CHECK-ACT) helps to provide a framework for structured and disciplined improvement activity.

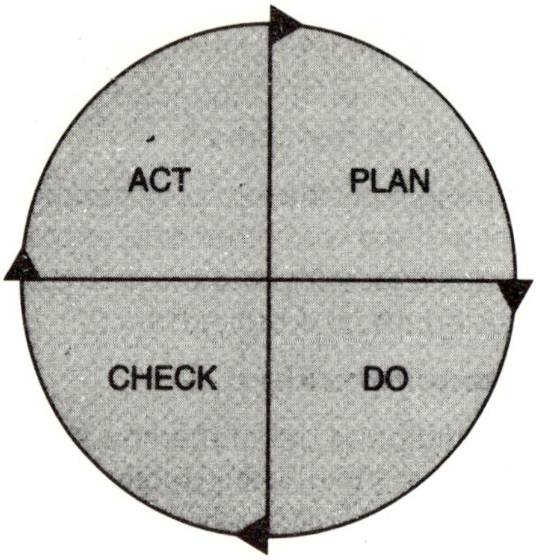

PLAN: Establish the facts.

Identify solution.

Prepare plan to implement the solution.

DO: Implement the solution.

CHECK: Monitor progress against plan.

ACT: Make successful solutions permanent.

The *Solve that problem!* Toolbox gives a full explanation of Plan–Do–Check–Act and the range of tools that is available at each step. The model is included here simply as a reminder of the value and importance of this discipline in bringing about effective change.

How to use it

PLAN

1. Select an opportunity for improvement

- Generate a list of opportunities for improvement.
- Before selection make sure all the possible options are identified.
- Prioritise and select an opportunity.

2. Identify the customer's requirements

- Specify the customer by name.
- Know and analyse the customer requirements.
- Be prepared to help the customer to define their requirements precisely.
- Develop a Customer-Supplier Agreement.

3. Define the problem

- How do the customer's requirements compare with the current situation?
- Describe the problem to be solved.

4. Collect data

- Define and map the current process.
- Select measurements needed: before, during and after the process.
- Collect data for analysis.

5. Analyse for root causes

- Do Cause and Effect Analysis and identify probable causes.
- Select the most probable causes and test if the root cause has been found.
- Define the root cause(s) of the problem.

6. Find solutions

- Develop criteria for solutions.
- Identify 'musts' versus 'wants'.
- Generate possible solutions, evaluate against the 'wants'/'musts' and select the best available solution.
- Do a Cost Benefit Analysis.

7. Prepare plan to implement solution

- Determine the expected improvement. Set specific objectives for improvement.
- Prepare initial action plan.
- Identify driving and restraining forces, using Force Field analysis and amend your plan accordingly.
- Finalise and agree the plan.
- Build in check points to monitor progress.
- If necessary gain approval to implement the solution.

> **HINT!** NOTICE THE NUMBER OF STEPS IN THE PLAN PART OF THE PROCESS COMPARED WITH THE DO, CHECK AND ACT PARTS OF THE QUALITY IMPROVEMENT CYCLE

DO

8. Implement the plan

- Carry out the plan, implement the solution.

CHECK

9. Monitor results – evaluate against plan

- Measure success against the customer's requirements and feedback.
- Is the customer delighted?
- What benefits can be measured?

- Monitor implementation against check points – do not wait until implementation is complete.

10. Determine reasons for deviations

- Where was the plan not successful?
- Ask why?

ACT

11. Corrective action for deviations

- Based on an understanding of why the plan was not successful, develop a revised plan.

12. Standardise the process – make the successful solutions permanent

- Make sure the gains that have been achieved are made permanent. (This is stabilising the improved process).

13. Reflect

- What have we learned? What have we achieved? What's our start point for further improvement?

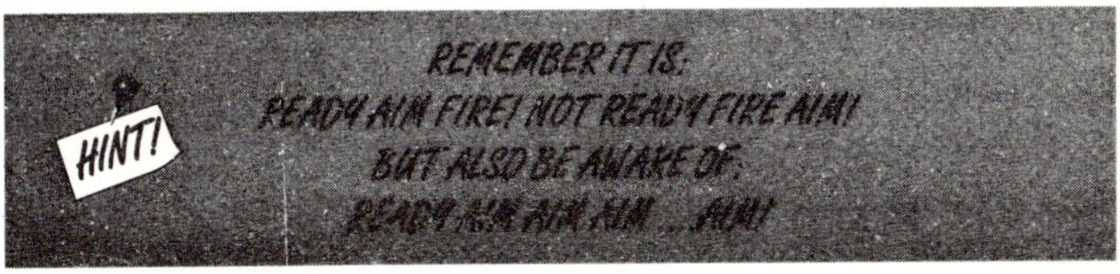

How it helps

The improvement process helps you solve problems and identify and implement solutions in a disciplined way. When all managers and staff use the same process, teamwork can be enhanced significantly.

Manage Risk-taking

What it is

Change inevitably involves trying new things – new machines, new software, new skills, new processes, etc. Change therefore involves uncertainty because new things are not always predictable; the environment can be turbulent and there can be a lack of information on which to base decisions. Inevitably therefore, change involves risk–taking, for example in terms of product quality, financial return, service performance or employee morale.

This tool gives some simple pointers on how you can manage risk–taking in order to maximise benefits and minimise problems.

How to use it

1. Review the checklist on 'managing risks'.
2. Reflect on the change you need to make.
3. What are the particular risks involved?
4. Which of the statements listed on the checklist will be most relevant to this particular change?
5. Brainstorm all of the things you could do to implement the suggested actions in your circumstances.
6. Develop a prioritised action plan to minimise the risks facing you.

Checklist for managing risks

✓ **Clarify objectives**

- Be clear what you need to achieve and how success will be measured
- Agree priorities where there are potentially conflicting demands on resources
- Be SMART – don't risk confusion and wasted resource

✓ **Agree boundaries/authority levels**

- Ensure individuals/teams know the limits of their authority and when they need to defer decisions
- Empower as much as possible but provide the practical support needed to ensure this is well used (see separate tool)
- Make it clear when you want others to take risks and be creative without leaving the consequences
- Regularly review appropriateness of authority levels, etc as processes develop and experience increases
- Don't risk stupid decisions

✓ **Regularly review**

- Agree metrics and methods to track performance
- Regularly review individual and team results and tackle corrective action quickly
- Don't risk getting out of touch and missing early signals of problems

✓ **Provide support to others**

- Coach, counsel, train and develop individuals and teams as needed
- Don't treat everyone the same – their needs will vary

- Don't risk poor performance and mistakes, through lack of personal development

✔ **Communicate**

- Keep everyone informed of what change is happening, why, how, when, where and who
- Provide regular updates, particularly if objectives or priorities change; performance is off–track or unforeseen problems arise

- Don't risk misguided actions through lack of information

✔ **Build support for change**

- Consult others for view and ideas. Test your plans.
- Seek consensus through involvement and clear communications
- Enlist specific supporters to sponsor, take part or facilitate the change

- Don't risk resistance or even sabotage through lack of buy in

✔ **Use teams**

- Broaden the skills and experience involved
- Use multi–disciplined teams to ensure a process view
- Apply project disciplines to focus and accelerate change

- Don't risk functional or narrow bias or slow action by relying completely on individuals

✔ **Use tools and discipline**

- Use problem-solving tools to increase objectivity (cost–benefit analysis; decision charts, etc)
- Apply PLAN–DO–CHECK–ACT to ensure adequate planning, analysis and follow through
- Don't risk purely emotional or ill thought out actions through lack of discipline

✔ **Research**

- Test your market. What do your customers really need? What do they think of the proposed change?
- Test your product in realistic conditions – does it work accurately? consistently? reliably?
- Watch your competitors – don't risk being left behind
- Follow your market and environment – don't be caught out by unexpected economic, political or social changes
- Don't risk wasting effort on things your customer won't pay for

✔ **Have contingencies**

- Develop back-up plans
- Ask 'what if...' questions
- Spread risk over time/locations/products, etc if appropriate
- Test 'disaster recovery' plans
- Ensure everyone knows what the contingencies are
- Don't risk being caught with no alternative when something fails

✔ **Use trials/test/pilots**

- Try out new products/processes/organisations, etc in a limited way
- Limit investment until it is clear that things work
- Don't risk losing large investments if you can reduce the risk by trying out change with smaller investment

✔ **Be bold**

- Be prepared to ignore the rest of this checklist if it seems the right thing to do
- Assess risks and if you can live with the consequences (what's the worst thing that can happen?...), just do it!
- Beware of smothering initiative and creativity in too much 'cotton wool' or losing a competitive edge through delay
- Keep focused on the prize to be had and not the potential pitfalls ahead
- Don't risk becoming a dinosaur by avoiding risk completely!

How it helps

Risk is inevitably part of change. By applying the strategies outlined in this tool you can help to minimise the risks and maximise the likelihood of gaining the benefits of the change you need to make.

9 Build energy and momentum

Use Facts

What it is

One of the most powerful methods of influencing individuals to make or accept change is to present them with hard facts to either support or deny their perceptions, expectations or assumptions.

This tool outlines when this is particularly useful and the types of information that can be used.

How to use it

1. Before any planned change takes place it is important to establish 'WHERE YOU ARE NOW'

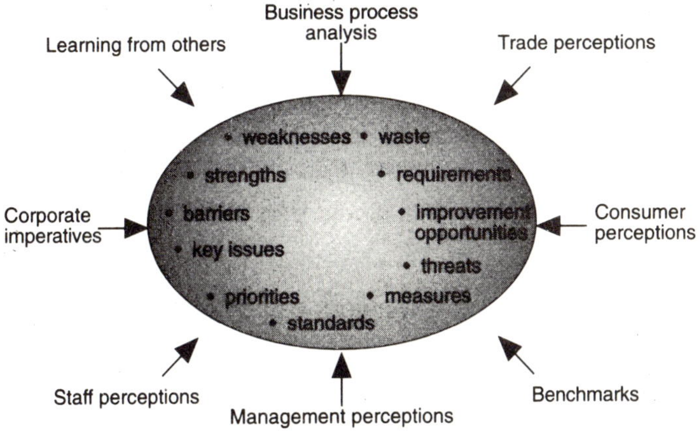

Typical data needs

Perception is reality but reality is rarely perception.

While the content of this will vary depending on the type of change, research can cover:

✔ **Customers**

- Who are they?
- What do they want? (product, service, cost, timescales, etc)
- How satisfied are they?
- What are their priorities?
- How do you compare against your competitors?
- What improvements would they like?

✔ **Suppliers**

- Who are they?
- What do they need from you? (information, access, samples, payment, etc)
- How satisfied are they?
- How do you compare to their other customers?
- What improvements would they like?

✔ **Employees**

- How do they feel about issues such as leadership, environment, processes, customers, communication, improvement activities, recognition?
- What improvements would they like?

✔ **Markets**

- What are your competitors doing? (who, what, how, prices, etc)
- What are the overall economic cycles? (spending, saving, building, consumption, etc)
- What new product innovations are due?

✔ Internal processes

- What are the activities, tasks that take place?
- How much time do they take?
- How efficient/productive are they?
- What do they cost?
- How accurate, complete, consistent are they?
- What measures are available?

2. In the light of the type of change you want to make, review the checklist above and identify:

- what information would be helpful?
- who will you present it to? (This influences the type, level and presentation of information)
- how will you collect it? (Internal/external resources; written telephone surveys; interviews; discussion groups; desk research, etc)?
- how will you analyse it?
- how will you present it?

3. Once change is underway there will probably come a time when:

- energy and enthusiasm are slipping
- resource has been used but the return is unclear
- the pace of change is slowing
- people start to question what's happening/value, etc.

At this point (it can be weeks, months or even years into the process depending on the scale of the change) it is useful to repeat the initial fact-find in order to identify:

- changes in satisfaction levels

- changes in needs
- changes in efficiency/effectiveness
- specific results/returns
- feedback on how to make change more effective.

4. Using this data you can then go on to develop a forward action plan which:

- is based on reality not perceptions/assumptions
- is targeted on the areas of greatest need
- is most likely to increase your competitive position in the market
- has buy-in from those who contributed data.

Increasingly organisations gather data on their performance against an external model such as the European Quality Award framework. This ensures a comprehensive picture and allows comparison with other organisations.

The European Quality Award framework:

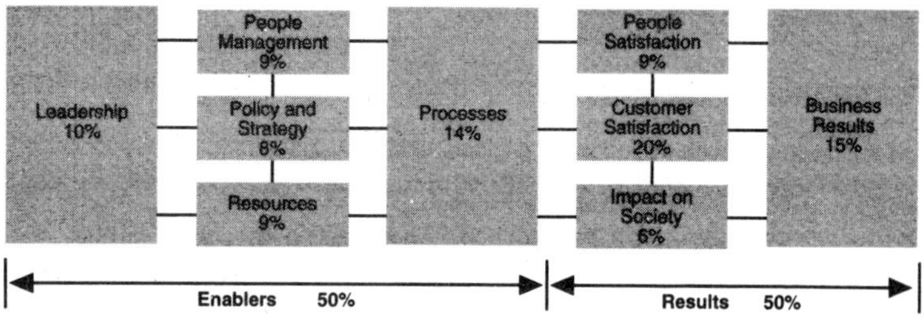

How it helps

It is difficult to argue with facts (when this happens refer to the tool on Handling Resistance).

Facts can help to initiate and energise change and then rekindle enthusiasm if and when it starts to wane. This tool outlines the type of facts that can be used and gives some pointers on their collection and presentation.

Generate Enthusiasm

What it is

Without energy, change will be slow and tedious and unlikely to achieve significant results.

This tool outlines a range of methods to generate enthusiasm and energy in an organisation and how to choose the most appropriate.

How to use it

1. Review the checklist on how to generate enthusiasm and energy.
2. In the light of the type of change you are trying to achieve, identify which of the methods listed would be most appropriate.
3. Discuss your views and ideas with those who will need to be involved and/or be directly affected.
4. Develop an action plan to take your ideas forward.

How to generate enthusiasm:

✔ **Communicate your vision and overall goals**

- Share your ambitions and dreams of the future
- Allow others to contribute or define the implications for them

✔ **Involve people in planning**

- Define the goals but delegate the means of achieving them to the appropriate level

✔ **Share information**

- As far as is possible, let people know how the organisation is performing

For example:

- financial situation
- customer feedback
- competitor analysis

- Keep everyone up to date as the situation changes

✔ **Seek views and ideas**

- Use an employee survey and/or discussion groups to allow people to speak up
- Introduce an OFI (Opportunities for Improvement) scheme so everyone can submit ideas
- Introduce regular team briefing meetings to ensure ongoing two way communication
- Act on what you hear or you won't be taken seriously

✔ **Use 'events' to bring people together**

- Use briefings, training, meetings as forums for debate; sharing and open discussion
- Encourage 'visits' between internal customers and suppliers to review needs

✔ **Use 'campaigns', 'themes', 'promotions'**

- Relaunch established programmes with new events and branding to remind people of key principles
- Develop next steps or add–ons to take programmes forward
- Ensure consistency and continuity with what has gone before to avoid criticism of 'flavour of the month'.

✔ **Develop new skills**

- Introduce individuals to new knowledge, skills and situations, for example, by becoming facilitators

✔ **Bring in new blood**

- Bring in outsiders or change around roles team membership internally to introduce fresh eyes and new ideas

✔ **Review progress to date**

- Survey interested parties (customers, suppliers, employees, managers)
- Communicate results widely – both good and bad
- Use results to develop forward action plans

How it helps

Energy is the key ingredient in making change happen. This tool identifies some practical ways of generating energy and enthusiasm to overcome the initial inertia and get things moving.

Identify Forces

What it is

This tool builds on forcefield analysis* by involving a group very actively in identifying the driving and resisting forces at work in a particular change situation. By quantifying these forces and prioritising them, the group can turn a seemingly stalemate situation into one of constructive action.

(*See the *Solve that problem!* Toolbox for details).

How to use it

1. Assemble a group of people involved in the particular change.
2. Break the group into two random halves.
3. Name one half 'The Drivers' and the other 'The Resistors'
4. Develop a large wall chart as big as possible (ideally covering a whole side of a room).

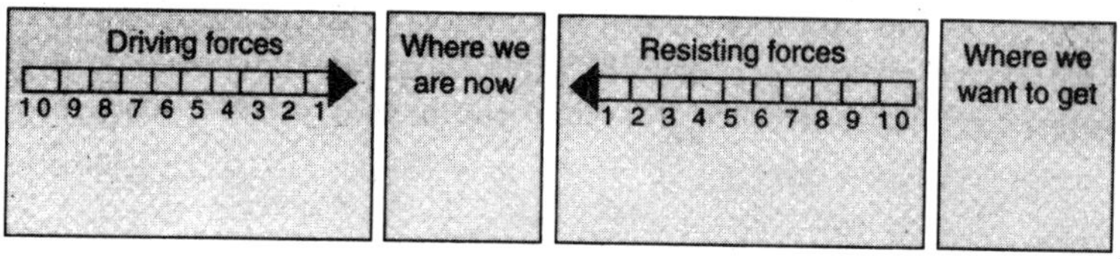

5. Start by completing the 'where we want to get to' and 'where we are now' boards. Encourage the expression of different views and ideas but aim for consensus.
6. Ask the Resistors to name a reason why this change will be difficult. Ask them to draw it up on the resisting forces chart showing its strength (1= slight, unlikely to have much impact, 10 = major, will sabotage or jeopardise success).

7. Ask the Drivers to name a force that will help bring change about. Again, ask for its strength on the scale.

   1 = will only marginally increase chance of success

   10 = major contributor to success.

8. Repeat the process until both teams have exhausted their ideas (try and keep the groups standing and moving so the exercise itself is dynamic).

9. Once all the forces have been identified, involve the two teams in developing action plans to build on the strongest drivers and minimise the strongest resistors.

How it helps

This tool gives a structured and enjoyable process for drawing out views on the forces which can both create and overcome blockages and encourage the development of action plans to overcome them.

Encourage Creativity

What it is

Creativity is the process of generating new ideas. While we may not all see ourselves as budding inventors or innovative thinkers there are some very practical things we can do to help ourselves and others to increase our creativity.

This tool outlines a range of actions which together will help to open up your mind.

How to use it

1. Review the ideas on how to encourage creativity below.
2. Identify the things you feel you already do. Be specific. Give examples.
3. Identify the areas you've never thought of tackling. Which ones appeal to you most?
4. How could you put them into practice in your work or your area?
5. Be creative in how you go about it.

HINT! REMEMBER: IF YOU ALWAYS DO WHAT YOU'VE ALWAYS DONE YOU'LL ALWAYS GET WHAT YOU'VE ALWAYS GOT

How to encourage creativity

✓ **Clarify objectives**

- Lift your eyes to your ultimate goal; focus on the benefits; imagine what it will be like
- Be honest and realistic about measures, constraints and resources, but see these as opportunities to do things differently

- Be demanding – it can force a new approach to working smarter not harder

✔ **Set groundrules**

- Agree when it's OK to take risks; make changes
- Clarify if and when you expect new ideas
- Remove existing norms if appropriate, (eg a proposal must always be cost justified before being presented)
- Take calculated risks to give freedom for innovation

✔ **Manage the environment**

- Move away from the 'normal' work environment
- Use colours, music, smells to generate ideas
- Create quiet 'thinking' places
- Make work fun and enjoyable (as well as demanding); too much stress and tension reduce creativity
- Encourage breaks – fresh air, movement and exercise and healthy food can stimulate thinking

✔ **Use mixed media**

- People respond differently to different methods
- Don't always rely on words to stimulate others
- Use pictures, sounds, touch to get across messages or to receive ideas
- Work with emotions as well as logical thoughts

✔ **Suspend your judgement**

- Be open–minded to new ideas
- Listen
- Develop others' ideas before assessing them

- Look for positives, not just problems (listen out for 'yes but...')
- Don't expect others to think or to express themselves as you do

✔ **Use problem solving tools**

- Use brainstorming and mind-mapping to open up possibilities
- Use the other tools in the *Solve that problem!* Toolbox to analyse options and plan actions

✔ **Use teams**

- Create a supportive yet demanding culture to encourage free expression and exploration
- Ensure members challenge the assumptions and perceptions of others
- Share experiences to broaden horizons
- Combine knowledge and skills to open up new ways
- Hold 'what if' meetings to imagine an alternative future
  - identify options, implications and impact
  - clarify what resources would be needed
  - assess the benefits
  - test ideas (where, how, what etc)
  - only reject ideas at the point you're sure they won't work.

✔ **Challenge paradigms**

- Use benchmarking to challenge assumptions about what can be done
- Visit other sites/departments/industries, etc to see different approaches
- Move people around to encourage a 'fresh pair of eyes'

- Stop and analyse the values, prejudices and assumptions that you (and others) have which colour your judgement... test whether they are appropriate

✔ **Think 'actively'**

- Don't just accept 'facts' passively (like watching the TV)
- Push yourself to think of alternatives; see things from the opposite point of view: do things a different way
- Make comparisons to highlight patterns, similarities or differences
- Learn to learn – set yourself development goals; take on new challenges; review yourself; seek feedback

✔ **Think positively**

- Have confidence in your ability to innovate
- Use your power to the full
- Believe in your own abilities and strengths – identify what they are and how you can build on them
- Have a 'can do' approach to problems, 'if you think you can, you will'
- Be 'out there' – getting out and about and making yourself available for people to raise questions/issues – **THEN** picking them up and getting them answered/dealt with – proactive facilitation if you like!
- Pick up on 'wild/off the wall ideas' – get in touch with the 'irrational'. Encourage people to bring these ideas to you, develop them with them, create something doable from them

- Don't ask why; ask why not! Dream it, do it, involve people

✔ **Learn from mistakes**. Ask yourself:

- what happened?
- why?
- what were/are the implications?
- what could be different next time?

How it helps

You can't have a new brain (yet!), but you can develop the one you've got to be more creative. This tool gives a range of practical actions you can take to increase your and others' creativity.

Capture Ideas (OFI)

What it is

Given the chance, everyone can come up with ideas on what and how things could be improved. They may not always know in detail how to go about it or be equipped to do so, but through their experiences, observations and frustrations they can readily point to the opportunities for improvement.

Improvement programmes usually include some form of OFI (Opportunities for Improvement) scheme which is specifically designed to give everyone the chance to speak up and receive feedback on their ideas.

An effective OFI process:

- Encourages everyone to speak up about opportunities for improvement (not necessarily solutions).
- Makes it easy to log these ideas for consideration.
- Ensures every idea is considered to identify if it should be progressed or actioned, and if so when and by whom.
- Ensures the individual or team who raised the OFI gets prompt feedback on what has been decided.
- Tracks the benefits achieved from implementing OFIs.
- Where appropriate, ensures OFIs which need project teams to progress them are transferred to the project management system.
- Provides data for communication to others on what is happening and benefits and for recognition of those involved.
- Ensures that improvement activity is focused on the goals and priorities of the unit.

- Ensures that all of this happens in a timely, disciplined and controlled way.

Benefits of an OFI system

- Wide participation and involvement in improvement.
- 'Bottom up' as well as 'top down' ideas are considered.
- Measures of involvement and achievements.
- Prioritised and focused actions.
- Resource control.

How to use it

Introducing an OFI process:

The following elements need to be considered in introducing an OFI process:

1. The system itself. Should it be:

- Local/company-wide?
- Paper/electronic?

2. Roles

- Who will administer?
- Who will make decisions?
- Who will maintain system/database?

3. Briefing/training

- How to ensure widespread awareness of the purpose of the scheme and how it operates?
- How to ensure everyone (on an ongoing basis) is able to use the system?

4. Measures

- What criteria will be used to assess OFI?
- How will the overall process be tracked, eg % participation, results/benefits, turnaround times?

- When and how will measures be reviewed?

5. Communication

- How will these measures and specific OFIs be communicated to a wide audience in a timely way, eg newsletters, board, team briefings?

6. Recognition

- How will the raising of OFIs and their successful implementation be recognised?
- Does this need clear guidelines and criteria?

7. Resource

- Having identified all the elements required – is there sufficient resource available?

How it helps

A well designed and implemented OFI scheme can be a very significant source of ideas for improvement. It can also energise and enthuse individuals who may (for the first time) feel that they wish to contribute their ideas and are able to do so.

Use Mind Mapping

What it is

A mind map is a way of generating and collating ideas and information that is:

- quick to do and use
- non–linear
- pictorial as well as verbal
- more interesting and colourful than text alone
- focused on relationships between ideas.

Mind maps can therefore increase creativity and energy by attracting and involving individuals who think visually and by providing a quick and enjoyable method of generating and assimilating ideas which can increase the enthusiasm of those involved.

How to use it

1. Identify the topic to be covered.
2. Write this in the middle of a large board or piece of paper.
3. Brainstorm the main elements or attributes of the topic. Add each to the mind map as a main branch.
4. For each branch, brainstorm its component parts and add these to the appropriate branch.
5. Whenever possible use pictures, symbols or charts instead of words.
6. Use different colours for different branches so they can be clearly differentiated.
7. If appropriate draw in links between branches and twigs.
8. Review your mind map for completeness and clarity

9. Once completed your map can be used to:

- store information/ideas for future reference
- communicate the output to others
- spark debate about issues and relationships between elements
- develop linear action plans, ie order of priorities, time scales, etc.

For example: the contents of this Toolbox were originally identified using a combination of brainstorming and mind-mapping:

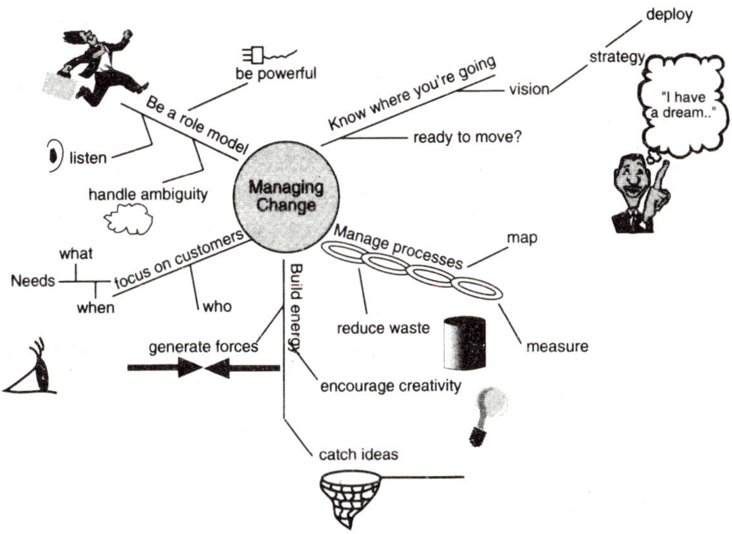

How it helps

Mind-space mapping is a fun way of involving people in generating ideas, capturing thoughts and demonstrating the relationships and connections between them; it appeals to visual thinkers as well as those more comfortable with words and avoids the trap of getting into linear thought processes too early.

Handle Resistance

What it is

Change rarely happens smoothly and easily. There are always reasons for some people to hang on to the 'old way' and even those who accept the need for change create blockages through a lack of knowledge or skill in how to go about it.

This tool outlines the typical reasons for resistance, the symptoms you may observe and how to confront them.

General sources of resistance are:

- Ignorance: due to a lack of information or understanding
- Disagreement: because alternative solutions are preferred or there are feelings that the plan will not work
- Personal cost: the effects on individuals are unwanted
- Anxiety: there is uncertainty as to how to do what is required or how to handle the situation
- Loss of authority: individuals wil lose power or control
- Mistrust: there is suspicion over motives or real objectives
- Alienation: individuals do not share the proposed vision/values or feel socially isolated
- Reward (or lack of it) 'What's in it for me' has not been addressed

How to use it

1. Listen carefully to the words you hear and the behaviours you see.
2. Try at least twice to answer the questions asked or issues raised at face value.
3. Use the following checklist to identify the form of resistance you are experiencing.

Some examples of resistance and suggested responses:

Behaviour	***Response***
Too busy	'You seem to be worried about the allocation of your time to this project'.
Refuses to share tasks	'You seem unwilling to draft the notice announcing this project to the department' (or whatever).
Compliance	'I can't tell what your real feelings are about this'.
Access to information	'You are not letting me (...interview the Chairman.) That cuts me off from essential information'.
Silence	'You are very quiet. I don't know how to read that'.
Pressing for early solutions	'It's too early for solutions. I'm still trying to find out...'.
Attack	'You don't seem to like me asking these questions'.
Nit-picking	'We're getting into too much detail'.

Avoidance of responsibility	'You don't seem to see yourself as part of the problem'.
Flooding with detail	'You are giving me more detail than I need. How could you describe it in a short statement?'
One word answers	'One word answers are not giving me enough, could you say more?'
Changing the subject	'I'd like to stay focused on one subject for a while'.
Asking for more detail	'Is this really necessary at this stage?'
References to the 'real world'	'You seem concerned about my approach'.

4. If resistance continues, name the behaviour in descriptive, non-evaluative language. If appropriate, state how you feel about it, again descriptively.

5. Be quiet, so that the concerns can surface and be heard.

6. Welcome resistance – it leads you to the deeper, underlying concerns. You cannot work well without knowing about them.

Remember

✔ Trust what you see more than what you hear. Pay attention to the non-verbal messages, they are much harder to fake

✔ Listen to yourself - when you feel uneasy, unclear or uncertain this may be an early sign of resistance

✔ Repetition and telltale phrases are signs of resistance

✔ Name the behaviour you observe

✔ Be silent. Don't speculate on the reasons

✔ Your silence will press him/her to give reasons

How it helps

Blockages and resistance are rarely overt. More often they are disguised and it is only over a period of time that their existence becomes apparent. This tool outlines what to look for and how to confront it.